# Qatar
## VISITORS' GUIDE

there's more to life...
ask**explorer**.com

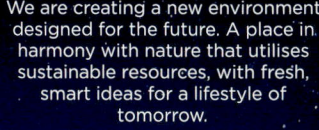

We are creating a new environment designed for the future. A place in harmony with nature that utilises sustainable resources, with fresh, smart ideas for a lifestyle of tomorrow.

This place is called Lusail.
Your home for the future.

For advance information visit:
**www.lusail.com**

THE ART OF REAL ESTATE

DEVELOPMENT & INVESTMENT. WORLDWIDE.

**Qatar Visitors'** Guide / 2nd Edition
ISBN – 978-9948-22-284-2

Copyright © Explorer Group Ltd 2014
All rights reserved.

All maps © Explorer Group Ltd 2014

Front cover photograph: Doha Corniche – Gary McGovern

Printed and bound by
Emirates Printing Press, Dubai, UAE

**Explorer Publishing & Distribution**
PO Box 34275, Dubai, United Arab Emirates
Phone (+971 4) 340 8805   Fax (+971 4) 340 8806
info@askexplorer.com
askexplorer.com

While every effort and care has been made to ensure the accuracy of the information contained in this publication, the publisher cannot accept responsibility for any errors or omissions it may contain.

No part of this publication may be reproduced, stored in a retrieval system, or transmitted, in any form or by any means, electronic, mechanical, photocopying, recording or otherwise, without the prior permission in writing of the publisher.

# Welcome...

Welcome to the *Qatar Visitors' Guide*. This mini marvel has been passionately prepared by the same team that brought you the *Qatar Residents' Guide*. Written by local residents, and perfect for visitors, you'll find all you need to make the most out of your time in this interesting country – whether you're looking for the top restaurants, the most stylish shops or the best cultural spots.

Qatar is a thriving, cosmopolitan country in the heart of the Middle East. The last few years have seen a staggering amount of development as the city of Doha has been transformed into a business hub and tourist hotspot. Explorer brings you insider knowledge of the sights and sounds of Qatar, from the traditional souks and the modern metropolis of Doha to the world-renowned museums and sports stadiums. Beyond the capital, there are impressive destinations to explore – from the rugged desert landscape to the fort-littered coasts.

For more information about Qatar and the GCC, plus up-to-the-minute events and exciting new releases from Explorer, log onto **askexplorer.com**, where you can also give us your own take on this unique country.

There's more to life...
**The Explorer Team**

   ask**explorer**.com

# Contents

## Essentials — 2
- Welcome To Qatar — 4
- Culture & Heritage — 6
- Modern Qatar — 16
- Qatar Checklist — 20
- Best Of Qatar — 30
- Visiting Qatar — 32
- Local Knowledge — 36
- Media & Further Reading — 42
- Public Holidays & Annual Events — 44
- Getting Around — 50
- Places To Stay — 56

## Exploring — 68
- Explore Qatar — 70
- Al Sadd & Al Rayyan Road — 72
- Al Dafna & West Bay — 76
- Doha Corniche — 82
- Khalifa Street & Al Luqta Street — 88
- Salwa Road & Al Aziziyah — 92
- Souk Area & Souk Waqif — 98
- Outside of Doha — 104
- Tours & Sightseeing — 110

## Sports & Spas — 114
- Active Qatar — 116
- Spectator Sports — 130
- Spas — 138

## Shopping — 142
- Shopping In Qatar — 144
- Hotspots — 146
- Markets & Souks — 148
- Shopping Malls — 154
- Department Stores — 160
- Where To Go For... — 162

## Going Out — 166
- Dining Out — 168
- Entertainment — 172
- Venue Directory — 176
- Area Directory — 180
- Restaurants & Cafes — 186
- Nightlife Establishments — 220

## Index — 226

askexplorer.com

# Essentials

| | |
|---|---|
| Welcome To Qatar | 4 |
| Culture & Heritage | 6 |
| Modern Qatar | 16 |
| Qatar Checklist | 20 |
| Best Of Qatar | 30 |
| Visiting Qatar | 32 |
| Local Knowledge | 36 |
| Media & Further Reading | 42 |
| Public Holidays & Annual Events | 44 |
| Getting Around | 50 |
| Places To Stay | 56 |

**Essentials**

# Welcome To Qatar

**Welcome to Qatar, a country of contrasts; traditional charm and contemporary architecture blend to form the landscape we see today.**

Qatar's current growth, high-end developments and low crime rate have made it an attractive destination for a broad mix of international visitors. If you are touching down in this fascinating region for business or for pleasure, Qatar has a lot to offer. With year-round sunshine, golden beaches, outdoor activities and a fascinating culture, this is a prime tourist destination. Qatar has become known as a high-quality destination, appealing to high-income sectors such as luxury leisure tourism and the MICE market (meetings, incentives, conferences and exhibitions). In order to attract the high-end market, the government has engaged in a massive, multi-billion investment programme to develop Qatar's infrastructure. Similarly, major cultural projects have been completed and most of the big international hotel chains are already represented in Qatar; yet investment continues and a host of new hotels and resorts have emerged in recent years to cater for the anticipated growth in visitor numbers. In short, welcome to a nation that is rapidly opening up to the world, with spectacular mega-projects like The Pearl, the critically acclaimed Museum of Islamic Art, mystical old souks full of hidden surprises, grandiose, bustling supermalls, beguiling deserts and endless charming beaches. Qatar also boasts a furiously developing sports scene that has led to the successful staging of the Asian Games in 2006 and the 2011 AFC Asian Cup. At the end of 2010, Qatar won the bid to host the 2022 FIFA Football World Cup – its most impressive victory to date. While the infrastructure plans to accommodate the huge surge of visitors expected to land in Qatar are vague at the moment, it's likely that the entire city will see impressive change over the coming years. Already, no fewer than nine stadiums are scheduled for development within the city limits.

The majority of Qatar's population resides in the capital city, Doha. Other major towns in the country include Mesaieed, Dukhan, Al Khor, Al Shamal and Al Wakra. Doha's mix of high-rise buildings, traditional and contemporary architecture brings with it a variety of experiences for visitors, whether it is a picturesque stroll around the Corniche or a spot of retail therapy at its comprehensive shopping malls and souks. Culture vultures will find solace in its art galleries and forts, while thrill seekers can venture outside of the city and participate in dune bashing and off-roading tours out towards the Inland Sea.

The following pages will help you familiarise yourself with Qatar. This chapter provides you with a solid background on Qatar's culture, history and current standing. The best spots to meet and eat are listed in Going Out, and you can find the best places to unwind, get active or release some tension in the Sports & Spas chapter. Discover Qatar's rich heritage and fascinating traditions, from Doha Corniche to Souk Waqif, in the Exploring chapter.

# Culture & Heritage

**Essentials**

**From its early ties to the expansion of Islam to its staggeringly rapid modern development, Qatar's history is rich.**

## Early Days

Archaeologists have uncovered evidence of human habitation in Qatar possibly dating back to the fourth and fifth millennia BC. In the fifth century BC the Greek historian Herodotus referred to the ancient Canaanites as the original inhabitants of Qatar. The country features on old maps of the region, suggesting that Qatar was already well-known to seafarers and traders of these early days.

Since Islam swept the region in the seventh century AD, Qatar's history has been forever linked to the religion. The inhabitants of Qatar are said to have aided the formation of the first Islamic naval fleet, a supposition aided by Qatar's maritime traditions such as pearl fishing.

## Growing Trade

Coinciding with the development and rapid expansion of Islam, Qatar also became well known for the quality of its textile manufacturing (especially cloaks) and for the making of arrow heads. In addition to a blossoming pearl fishing industry, this effectively marked the beginning of what was to become a significant trading hub. In the 13th and 14th centuries, Qatar enjoyed a favourable relationship with the Caliphates (successors of the Prophet Muhammad) in

*Traditional fort in Al Wakra*

Essentials

Culture & Heritage

Baghdad and it became an important centre for pearl trading. Evidence from this Abbasid era (Caliphate rule) can be seen in the architecture of Murwab Fort on Qatar's west coast. In the 16th and 17th centuries the Portuguese were a powerful force throughout the Gulf region. To protect itself from occupation and aggression, Qatar aligned with the Turks. This saw the start of over three centuries of rule by the Ottoman Empire, although throughout this period the real power in Qatar always remained with the local sheikhs.

The ancestors of today's ruling family, the Al Thanis, arrived in Qatar in the early 18th century. Originating from a branch of the Bani Tamin tribe from Najd in modern-day Saudi Arabia, they first settled in southern Qatar before moving to the north of the peninsula in the mid 1700s. Qatar, and especially the northern town of Zubarah, continued to be a key centre for the pearl trade during this time.

# Independence

In the mid 19th century, Sheikh Mohammed bin Thani established Al Bidda, the modern city of Doha, as the capital and seat of power. Soon after, in 1868, a treaty negotiated with the British recognised him as the first official Emir of Qatar. This treaty signed with the British also recognised Qatar's independence. Three years later, Sheikh Mohammed signed another treaty with the Turks, accepting protection against external attack. A Turkish garrison was established in Doha, but the relationship was an uneasy one and the Ottomans were forced to abandon Doha in 1915. In 1916, Sheikh Abdullah Al Thani signed a further treaty with the

British promising not to enter into relations with any other power without prior consent. In return, Britain guaranteed the protection of Qatar 'from all aggression by sea'. A number of factors, including worldwide economic depression and the introduction of cultured Japanese pearls, led to an almost complete collapse of the Gulf's pearling industry in the 1930s. Pearling had been the mainstay of Qatar's economy for generations, and while life for the country's inhabitants had never been easy, this development was a desperate blow. The region was plunged into dire poverty and disease was rife among the undernourished people.

## The Discovery Of Oil

In the midst of economic hardship in the young country's early days, there was hope though: the discovery of oil. Qatar's neighbouring island nation Bahrain had become the first Gulf state to strike oil earlier in the decade and, in 1935, Sheikh Abdullah signed the first Oil Concession Agreement with the Anglo-Persian Oil Company. Drilling began and oil was discovered in Dukhan in 1939. The onset of the second world war slowed down the process and the first oil wasn't exported from Qatar until the next decade. The discovery of vast natural resources has transformed the lives of the population beyond recognition, as the rulers set about modernising the country's infrastructure and creating healthcare and education facilities. The wealth generated from oil exports and the discovery of the world's largest single reservoir of natural gas means that Qatar today enjoys the highest level of income per capita in the world.

## Culture

Qatari culture is an interesting mix of traditional Islamic values and western influence. Islam influences day-to-day living, from the clothes Muslims wear to particular features of the local cuisine and diet. On the surface, one of the first things a visitor notices is the Qatari national dress – long, white dishdashas for men and elegant, flowing black abayas for women. The clothing acts as a constant reminder that, although Qatar's developments are propelling it into a globalised future, the country will always hold on to its rich heritage.

Generally speaking, Qatar is a tolerant and welcoming country with few restrictions placed on visitors and expat residents. For example, women are not required to cover up completely in public (although it is a good idea to dress relatively conservatively, especially during Ramadan). Similarly, although public displays of affection are a cultural no-no, holding hands in public has become more acceptable in recent years. Overall, visitors are likely to counter few, if any, issues: among the most highly prized values of Islam are courtesy and hospitality and visitors are likely to be charmed by the genuine warmth and friendliness of the local people.

## Food & Drink

Spending time in this region is an ideal opportunity to familiarise yourself with pan-Arabic cuisine. Street restaurants selling shawarma, falafel, tabbouleh, hummus and fresh fruit cocktails are a good place to start. Many of the most common Arabic delicacies originated in Lebanon and have been adopted by other parts of the Arab world. That's not to say other Arab countries don't have their own culinary heritage.

Traditional Qatari cuisine is heavily influenced by Indian and Iranian cooking and the country's central location has exposed it to spices and ingredients not found in other Arabian cuisines. Early traders introduced new spices and flavours that have become essential in Qatari cooking. Cinnamon, saffron, turmeric, nuts (especially almonds and

**Essentials**

pistachios), limes and dried fruits all add interesting flavours to well-known Qatari dishes like ghuzi, harees and machbous. See the Going Out chapter for listings of restaurants where you can sample local delicacies. Eating the Middle Eastern way is a social affair. Whether eating at home with extended families or out with large groups of friends, the custom is for everybody to share various dishes served in communal bowls. A combination of starters, known as mezze, is usually enjoyed with flat bread. The main courses often include a variety of grilled meats; various kebabs, koftas and shish ta'ooq (marinated boneless chicken) are among the most common mains you're likely to encounter at the table here. Kibbe, coated balls of burghul wheat stuffed with pine nuts, is another must for visitors looking for a truly local speciality.

## Arabian Coffee & Dates

Coffee and dates are an important ritual in this part of the world. Traditional Arabian style coffee (kahwa) is mild, with a distinctive taste of cardamom and saffron. It is served black without sugar, but dates are presented at the same time to sweeten the palate. It is polite to drink about three of the tiny cups if offered by a local host. In fact, to refuse the coffee is seen as a refusal of the host's generosity, so this should be avoided if possible. Shake the cup as a sign that you don't want another refill. Dates, one of the few crops that naturally thrive in the Middle East, have been cultivated in this region for around 5,000 years. High in energy, fibre and micro-nutrients that include various vitamins, magnesium and iron, dates are popular as a healthy, tasty snack.

## Shisha

Smoking a shisha pipe is an important part of socialising the authentic Middle Eastern way. It is often savoured in cafes while chatting with friends; many of the restaurants listed in Going Out serve shisha on their atmospheric terraces during the cooler months of the year. Sometimes also called 'hubbly-bubbly' or 'hookah,' shishas are filled with water, and the tobacco, which has a texture similar to molasses, is available in different flavours. Even if you don't smoke cigarettes or cigars, you shouldn't miss the chance to try shisha at least once; the smoke is 'smoothed' by the water, creating a much milder effect and even if you don't end up finishing the pipe, the experience is likely to linger in your memories of the trip here.

## Dietary Restrictions

Muslims are not allowed to eat pork, so you're less likely to find dishes containing pork products in most restaurants. In order for a venue to have pork on its menu, the kitchen needs to have a separate fridge, preparation equipment and cooking area for the handling of pork; as a result, it generally does not feature on menus very often. Alcohol is also considered haram (taboo) in Islam. It is only served in licensed outlets associated with hotels (restaurants and bars), plus a few leisure venues (such as golf clubs) and clubs. Restaurants outside of hotels, that are not part of a club or association, are not permitted to serve alcohol. However, as a visitor you'll have plenty of choice when it comes to watering holes – see the Going Out chapter for listings of bars and nightclubs in Qatar.

# Religion

For Qataris, Islam is more than just a religion, it is a way of life. Qataris are generally conservative and the majority practise their religion. The basis of Islam is that there is only one God and that Prophet Muhammad is the messenger of God. Islam is based on five pillars: profession of faith, praying, fasting, pilgrimage to Mecca in Saudi Arabia and giving to charity. Islam's holy book is the Quran. There are two main forms of Islam: Sunni and Shia. Almost 90% of Qataris are Sunni.

Islam requires believers to pray five times a day. Calls to prayer, which are reminders of the prayer times, are broadcast from loudspeakers installed on the minarets of the many mosques. Praying must be preceded by ritual cleansing, so washing facilities can be found in buildings and public places. Mosques are usually packed with mostly male worshippers on Fridays, when they get to listen to a sermon, or khotbeh, given by a preacher or imam.

## Ramadan

Fasting from sun up to sundown is observed for a whole month during Ramadan, which is the ninth month of the Islamic calendar; the exact timing is determined by the moon.

From a visitor's point of view, there are a few restrictions to bear in mind: first and foremost, as eating and drinking in public is prohibited during the day, most restaurants are closed until sundown (except for some in major hotels). Visitors should dress and behave modestly. Alcohol is not served during the holy month or on religious holidays.

*Prayer time at a local mosque*

## Essentials

# Modern Qatar

**With ample natural resources, Qatar has focused its future on arts and culture instead of glitz and glam.**

Fifty years ago, this tiny Gulf peninsula was only beginning to blossom – oil had just begun to be exported, and the region-leading healthcare and education projects that define the country were only in the planning stages. The Qatar of today may still rely on oil and natural gas to fuel its growing economy, but the country's physical landscape is hardly recognisable. Massive infrastructure projects have taken place over the past few decades and visitors to Qatar will now drive along plush roads lined up by towering skyscrapers where palms trees and beach huts once stood.

## People & Economy

Qatar's population has grown exponentially over the past few decades. Currently, the country is home to some 1.69 million people, around 80% of which are foreign nationals and expat workers from around the world. The Qatari statistic that most often captures the global headlines is the country's GDP per capita, which the International Monetary Fund (IMF) estimated at $106,000 in 2013. This puts Qatar in pole position in international comparisons. Yet this top-ranking purchasing power is just one part of the country's astonishing growth story: since the mid-1990s, when Emir Sheikh Hamad bin Khalifa Al Thani committed

Qatari nationals on the Corniche

to a development strategy that based his country's future on developing gas reserves, Qatar has gone from strength to strength. After initially borrowing billions to pay for its expensive energy infrastructure, Qatar has become the world's leading exporter of liquefied natural gas (LNG) and with some 15% of the world's LNG reserves, the prospects for further growth in this field remain bright. Buoyed by the petrochemical sector, Qatar's GDP expanded 18% in 2011. In 2013, economic growth accelerated to 6.5%, thanks to an increase in foreign workers and construction ahead of the FIFA World Cup in 2022.

**Essentials**

## Tourism

In contrast to some of its Gulf neighbours, Qatar doesn't necessarily want to attract mass tourism. Instead, it aims to attract high-end sectors. The country is emerging as a popular destination for cultural, educational and sports tourism, luxury leisure and the MICE market (meetings, incentives, conferences and exhibitions). In the first quarter of 2014, Qatar Tourism Authority revealed that the number of regional and international visitors to Qatar reached 387,000, representing a year-on-year increase of 9%. This reflects Qatar's continuing development as an attractive destination under the year-round Gulf sun.

## New Developments

The government is investing billions to prepare for the expected increase in visitor numbers and several massive development projects, ranging from infrastructure to hotels and leisure attractions, are either currently under way or in the process of being finalised. The average hotel occupancy rate has risen from 68% to 75%, according to the QTA report. The increased accommodation capacity is designed to match the expected inflow of visitors drawn in by the growing number of exhibitions held at the new Qatar International Convention Centre (open since late 2011), as well as the upcoming FIFA World Cup. Qatar's commercial airport, Doha International Airport, closed in May 2014. It has since been replaced by Hamad International Airport, which opened in April 2014. The latter is located a few minutes east of the previous site and is partially built on reclaimed land.

**Essentials**

**Essentials**

# Qatar Checklist

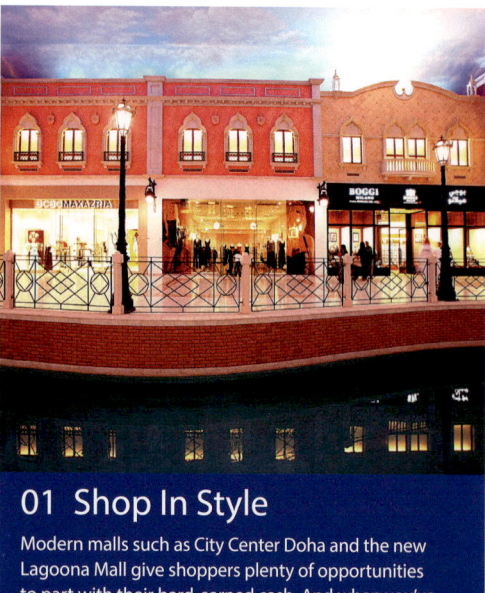

## 01 Shop In Style

Modern malls such as City Center Doha and the new Lagoona Mall give shoppers plenty of opportunities to part with their hard-earned cash. And when you've shopped till you're ready to drop, there's no end of cafes, restaurants and cinemas to help revive the weary.

Essentials

Qatar Checklist

## 02  Conquer The Corniche

Perhaps the most picturesque part of the capital, the Corniche extends seven kilometres in a horseshoe around Doha Bay. The area is a popular destination for walkers and joggers who take the opportunity to exercise outdoors, but there are plenty of places to sit back and enjoy the skyline or the night lights.

**Essentials**

Qatar Checklist

## 03  Step Back In Time

For a fascinating view of Qatar's history, escape from the city and travel north from Doha to Umm Salal Mohammed. You'll marvel at the ancient buildings and architecture, including the impressive fort and Barzan Tower.

## 04 Dine At The Pearl

Porto Arabia is setting the standard of high-end dining and shopping. Enjoy a stroll along the promenade, which is reminiscent of the Italian Riviera, before indulging in one of the many fabulous eateries around the Marina.

Essentials

Qatar Checklist

## 05  Visit The Museum Of Islamic Art

This is Qatar's pride and joy. Built on an island, this impressive landmark is an iconic addition to Doha's skyline. Wander through the exhibitions which cover over a thousand years of Islamic art.

## 06 Take A Dhow Cruise

This is a fabulous way to see Doha from the water. The best time to take the cruise is in the evening, so you can enjoy the sunset and witness the city's skyline by night. Evening cruises will often include dinner and drinks too.

Essentials

Qatar Checklist

## 07  Go Dune Bashing

Khor Al Adaid, also known as the 'Inland Sea', is at the south-eastern end of the country and requires a four-wheel drive and an experienced driver to reach. The towering dunes make it perfect for sand skiing or boarding and its calm waters are great for swimming.

## 08 Explore The Cultural Village Of Katara

Designed to recreate a large Qatari village, this new development has sparked a lot of cultural commotion around town, quickly becoming a popular leisure hub among local expats and visitors alike.

**Essentials**

**Qatar Checklist**

## 09 Shop At Souk Waqif

Souk Waqif is the oldest Arabian-style market in Qatar. You can, quite literally, lose yourself in the fascinating maze of alleyways, with their small shops selling anything and everything imaginable from pots and pans to clothing, spices, baskets, and perfumes.

**Essentials**

Qatar Checklist

## 10 Relax & Unwind In Rumeilah Park

Sometimes referred to by its old name, Al Bidda, this public park opposite the Corniche is popular in the evening and at weekends. It has lots of green space, cafes, and a heritage village.

# Best Of Qatar

## For Adrenaline Junkies

Qatar's geographic location lends itself well to thrilling explorations of the great outdoors. The desert surrounding Doha and the other urban areas provides a great deal of interest for those looking for a bit of adventure. A trip to the 'Inland Sea', which is also known as Khor Al Adaid, is a perfect excuse to get the adrenaline pumping, with a little help from a 4WD (SUV). As well as enjoying a bit of off-roading, dune bashing and sand boarding, you can experience the area's wildlife. It is important to venture out with an experienced driver. There are a few tour companies that offer off-roading trips out into the desert, which often include a night camping out among the dunes.

## For Big Spenders

Qatar's vast malls, plush hotels and spas offer no shortage of ways to spend some riyals. Begin your spree by staying at one of Doha's plush hotels offering a luxurious combination of palatial grounds, superior eateries and stylish bars. Then trot down to one of Doha's wide-ranging malls such as City Center Doha or Lagoona which offer a mix of high street brands, designer labels and electronics – and plenty to entertain kids while you satisfy your need for retail therapy. End the day with a bit of pampering at one of Doha's luxurious spas. The Spa at the Marriott Doha features Turkish baths to relax in, while the Six Senses Spa at Sharq Village & Spa offers 23 treatment rooms and a plunge pool.

## For Culture Buffs

There are a growing number of hotspots for those looking for a touch of culture in Qatar. The Waqif Arts Center is located in Souk Waqif and it houses some small galleries. The Cultural Village of Katara is not a traditional museum but rather a unique new development that brings together various artistic elements including music, theatre, photography, painting and art. The iconic Museum of Islamic Art features a broad variety of art spanning over three continents, from the seventh century to the present day. The latest opening, located in the impressive architecture of Education City, is the Mathaf Arab Museum of Modern Art which exhibits contemporary art from the Middle East's most famous artists. There are hands-on workshops, curatorial tours, film screenings and poetry readings that are all worth a look.

## For Water Babies

The region's clear and warm waters are the perfect environment for adrenaline seekers to enjoy watersports of all kinds. The Sealine Beach Resort and the Diplomatic Club both offer a good range of watersports. There is also a keen interest in diving in Doha, while the powerboat racing scene is growing each year. For those looking to take it easy during their stay, there are several resorts with beautiful beach facilities. Also, Qatar's first public beach is now open at Katara, where there are water inflatables to keep children amused and plenty of sun loungers for adults.

# Visiting Qatar

**Qatar is a welcoming country and, with excellent international traffic connections, getting there is easy.**

## Getting There

Hamad International Airport is located by the Gulf coast on Ras Abu Aboud Street and, traffic permitting, is readily accessible from anywhere in Doha in a maximum of 30 minutes. The airport is home to the constantly expanding national airline, Qatar Airways. With one of the youngest fleets of Airbus and Boeing aircraft in the world, Qatar Airways is continually adding new routes to add to an already impressive network of destinations in nearly all corners of the world. To cope with this growth drive and increased traffic, an expansion of the Doha airport is currently being finalised with expected completion in the next few years.

## From The Airport

Five and four-star hotels operate their own airport transfer services for their guests; you will see their desks as you leave the departures hall. Turn left outside the departures hall to find both Karwa Taxis and limousines. The airport taxi base charge is QR 18. You are also likely to be accosted by individuals offering private taxi services, but these are unofficial, unlicensed and best avoided. Public bus services from the airport are limited, with only the number 49 circular route heading towards town.

## Airlines

| | | |
|---|---|---|
| Air Arabia | 4407 3434 | airarabia.com |
| Air India | 4462 2544 | airindia.in |
| Bahrain Air | 4442 1807 | en.bahrainair.net |
| British Airways | 4432 1434 | ba.com |
| Cathay Pacific Airways | 4457 4000 | cathaypacific.com |
| Delta Airlines | 4483 0725 | delta.com |
| Egypt Air | 4435 6020 | egyptair.com |
| Emirates Airline | 4438 4477 | emirates.com |
| Etihad Airways | 800 5501 | etihadairways.com |
| Gulf Air | 4499 8000 | gulfair.com |
| Lufthansa | 4433 4000 | lufthansa.com |
| Qatar Airways | 4449 6000 | qatarairways.com |
| Royal Jordanian | 4443 1431 | rj.com |
| Saudi Arabian Airlines | 4444 0121 | saudiairlines.com |
| Singapore Airlines | 4499 5700 | singaporeair.com |
| Turkish Airlines | 4443 3027 | turkishairlines.com |

# Visas & Customs

Visa requirements for entering Qatar vary depending on your nationality and purpose of visit. Always check current regulations before travelling as details can change unexpectedly. Your passport must be valid for at least six months and have at least one blank page. GCC nationals (Bahrain, Kuwait, Oman, Saudi Arabia and UAE) do not need a visa prior to visiting Qatar. Citizens of 33 countries, including most European and North American countries as well as Australia, New Zealand and Hong Kong, are currently eligible for automatic visas on arrival. When you arrive, head to customs and your passport will be stamped with a 30 day renewable visit visa. It costs QR 100 and is payable by credit card only. You can visit the government website (gov.qa/wps/portal) and pre-order your visa online for QR 55 (tourist visa). You can extend your visit visa in person at the Department of Immigration (opposite the airport car park, open 24 hours). Just present your passport prior to the visa's expiration period and pay a QR 100 fee. A fine of QR 200 per day is applicable if you overstay your visa. All other nationalities can get a 30 day tourist visa, costing QR 200, from either a Qatar-based sponsor or by arrangement with one of the hotels. Recently, the Qatar Ministry of Interior published a revised list of 188 categories of professionals who can get a visa on arrival at the airport, if they are GCC residents. This visa is valid for one month and will only be issued if the traveller's GCC residency permit is valid for at least six months, as well as their passport. They will also need a return ticket. In early 2010, the Qatari government announced the end to visas on arrival for all nationalities, but this was later put on indefinite hold. For the latest regulations, check with your local Qatari embassy prior to travelling.

## Visitor Information In Qatar

For travel tips, experienceqatar.com and qatar-tourism.com are very good for basic information. The government also runs an English language web portal; to access, type 'Qatar Hukoomi' into your search engine. Once in Doha, the easiest way to get information is through your hotel's concierge.

Essentials

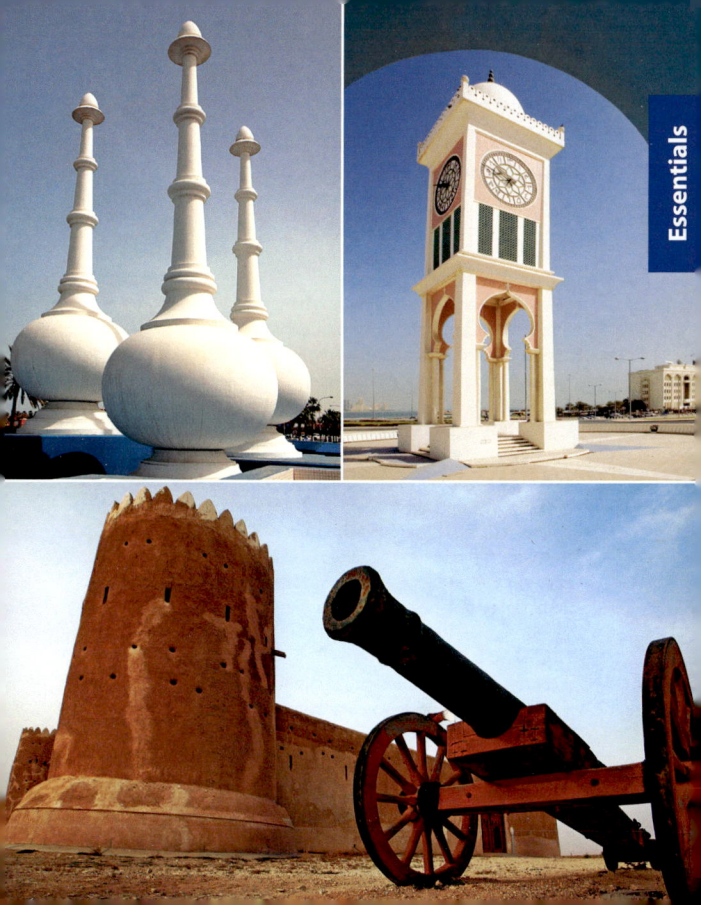

# Local Knowledge

**Progressive Qatar is an ideal destination to experience Middle Eastern culture in a thoroughly modern setting.**

## Climate
Qatar's climate is characterised by mild winters and very hot summers, with temperatures reaching over 40°C (104°F). Doha's winter, from late October until late March, is pleasant during both the day and evening. Rainfall is scarce, averaging 70mm per year, falling on isolated days in winter.

## Crime & Safety
Qatar is considered a safe country. The crime rate is much lower than in some western countries, but you should still take sensible precautions with valuables and cash and avoid unfamiliar areas especially when alone or at night. Perhaps the biggest danger to the safety of visitors is the standard of driving; accidents are commonplace, so expect the unexpected and be especially careful if out on foot.

## Dos & Don'ts
Although there is a tolerance of other cultures in Qatar, you should remember that you are visiting a Muslim country. Basic awareness of local customs will help you avoid any trouble. In order to respect the culture it's a good idea to dress conservatively. For women, wearing tight clothes, sleeveless shirts and short skirts in public is frowned upon

and these should be avoided. Public displays of affection between men and women are a no-no and can lead to arrest. Generally speaking, any form of contact between unmarried men and women is viewed unfavourably, so if in doubt when meeting a local of the opposite sex don't offer your hand unless it is offered first. Alcohol is only served in limited, licensed venues and should never be drunk openly in public outside of these establishments. Also, always remember that there is zero tolerance for drinking and driving – offenders may face detention, a substantial fine, a prison sentence or even deportation. Penalties for possession of drugs are severe, usually resulting in prison sentences.

## Electricity & Water

The electricity in Qatar is 240 volts and the sockets are of the three-pin (UK) type, although most appliances will have two-pin plugs, so stock up on adaptors. Tap water is perfectly safe to drink. However, most expat residents tend to prefer to drink mineral water, which you can either buy from the supermarket in boxes or have delivered in five-gallon bottles.

## Female Visitors

Women will face few problems or restrictions while in Qatar; female visitors are not required to wear covered clothing such as headscarves and are allowed to drive and travel freely (accompanied or alone). This said, local customs should be respected and female visitors should avoid tight or revealing clothing when outside of beach areas. If you receive some unwanted stares, it's best to simply ignore it.

# Language

The official language in Qatar is Arabic but English is so widely used that you'll find few difficulties getting by without any knowledge of Arabic. However, picking up a few words may at least earn you a smile when out and about.

## Basic Arabic

### General

| | |
|---|---|
| Yes | na'am |
| No | la |
| Please | min fadlak (m)/min fadliki (f) |
| Thank you | shukran |
| Praise be to God | al-hamdu l-illah |
| God willing | in shaa'a l-laah |

### Greetings

| | |
|---|---|
| Greeting (peace be upon you) | as-salaamu alaykom |
| Greeting (in reply) | wa alaykom is salaam |
| Good morning | sabah il-khayr |
| Good morning (in reply) | sabah in-nuwr |
| Good evening | masa il-khayr |
| Good evening (in reply) | masa in-nuwr |
| Hello | marhaba |
| Hello (in reply) | marhabtayn |
| How are you? | kayf haalak (m)/kayf haalik (f) |
| Fine, thank you | zayn, shukran (m)/zayna, shukran (f) |

# Essentials

| Welcome | ahlan wa sahlan |
|---|---|
| Goodbye | ma is-salaama |

## Introductions

| My name is... | ismiy... |
|---|---|
| What is your name? | shuw ismak (m) / shuw ismik (f) |
| Where are you from? | min wayn inta (m) / min wayn inti (f) |

## Questions

| How many / much? | kam? |
|---|---|
| Where? | wayn? |
| When? | mataa? |
| Which? | ayy? |
| How? | kayf? |
| What? | shuw? |
| Why? | laysh? |
| And | wa |

## Numbers

| Zero | sifr |
|---|---|
| One | waahad |
| Two | ithnayn |
| Three | thalatha |
| Four | arba'a |
| Five | khamsa |
| Six | sitta |
| Seven | saba'a |
| Eight | thamaanya |
| Nine | tiss'a |
| Ten | ashara |

Local Knowledge

## Money

The monetary unit of Qatar is the Qatari riyal (QR). It is divided into 100 dirhams (not to be confused with the UAE dirham, which has almost the same value as the Qatari riyal). Banknote denominations include QR 1, QR 5, QR 10, QR 50, QR 100 and QR 500. The coins that are most commonly found are 25 and 50 dirhams. One, five and 10 dirham coins are still legal tender but are rarely seen. The riyal is pegged to the US dollar at a rate of QR 3.65. Major shops, hotels and restaurants do take credit and debit cards, but cash is the preferred method of payment in smaller shops and the souks.

## People With Disabilities

Facilities for disabled travellers are improving rapidly throughout Qatar. Most five star hotels have rooms and facilities adapted for disabled guests and the airport has ramps and chair lifts available. Hamad International Airport's meet and greet service, Al Maha (4010 3446), will also offer assistance to disabled visitors.

## Police

The telephone number for the police (and all emergency services) is 999. The police are usually fairly quick to respond to a call. If you are involved in a minor traffic accident (that does not involve injury or major damage to the vehicle) you should move your vehicle to the side of the road, away from traffic, and wait until the police arrive. Police officers are generally courteous and professional, and always willing to offer assistance to visitors.

## Telephone & Internet

Qatar has over 800 public phones, which can be used for local and international calls using payphone cards that are available countrywide. Ooredoo also offers two calling cards, the Qcard that can be used from any telephone, payphone or mobile, and the Dawli International Cards that are available in denominations of QR 10, 25, 30, 50 and 75 and can be used from any Ooredoo mobile or landline. Hala is a pay-as-you-talk option. Hala SIM cards are available at Ooredoo offices, and the scratch-off recharge cards (with values of QR 30, QR 50, QR 100 and Qr 200) are widely available in shops, supermarkets and Ooredoo offices. Ooredoo Wi-Fi HotSpots are all over the city; for a list of locations, visit ooredoo.com.

## Time

Qatar local time is three hours ahead of UCT (Universal Coordinated Time – formerly known as GMT). It is fixed across the country and there is no summertime daylight saving. So when it is 12pm in Doha, it is 1pm in the UAE, 9am in London, 4am in New York and 6pm in Tokyo (not allowing for any daylight saving in those countries).

## Tipping

Tips are most commonly given in restaurants, averaging 10%, although some establishments automatically add a 10% service charge to the bill (this should be stated on the menu). Taxi fares are generally minimal so tips that round out dirhams or riyals are common. Tipping your tour guides is subjective, but is good practice.

## Newspapers & Magazines

The three main English newspapers available in Qatar are Gulf Times, Qatar Tribune and The Peninsula. They are all published every day, and cover a range of international and local issues. Each paper costs QR 2 and you can find them in supermarkets, shops, hotels, bookshops and they are also sold by street vendors at traffic lights. Foreign newspapers, mostly British, American and Asian, are also available, although some may only arrive at the newsstands a day after the publishing date. There are three local Arabic dailies issued in Qatar: Al-Raya, Al-Sharq and Al-Watan, which cost QR 2. Many of the major glossy magazines are available in Qatar, but if they're imported from the US or Europe, you can expect to pay at least twice the normal cover price. Alternatively, you can pick up the Middle East versions of a number of popular titles including Harper's Bazaar, Grazia and Hello! magazines. All international titles are examined and, where necessary, censored to ensure that they don't offend the country's moral codes.

## Television

There are two TV channels operated by Qatar Television – Channel One, which is in Arabic, and Channel Two, which is mostly in English. Ooredoo offers cable TV (Qatar Cablevision), which supplies all available networks with one decoder. The system has a range of programmes suitable for English and Arabic-speaking viewers, including STAR, Orbit, and Showtime, and there are various packages that bundle together TV options with broadband and telephone connections.

# Radio

There are only a few Qatar-based radio stations available. Qatar Radio (QBS) is the main station, which operates in both English and French on 97.5 FM and 102.6 FM. French programming is broadcast between 13:15 and 16:00. Arabic-speaking listeners can tune into Voice of the Gulf on 100.8 FM.

# Books & Maps

A listing of Qatar's events can be found in a free booklet called *Qatar Happening*, which is distributed in malls and hotels. Explorer's comprehensive *Qatar Residents' Guide*, provides detailed information about the country as well as a useful pull-out map. A locally published book Marhaba also offers detailed listings for residents in the country. Explorer's *Impressions Qatar* is a coffee table photography book that captures the essence of the country, while *Doha Mini Map* is a handy, pocket-sized map that will help you navigate your way around the city.

## Websites & Blogs

| | |
|---|---|
| experienceqatar.com | Photos, events, news, brochures |
| gov.qa | Qatar government online |
| thepeninsulaqatar.com | News, economic information |
| qatarliving.com | What's on and community forum |
| qatartourism.gov.qa | Qatar information |
| aljazeera.com | Qatar and world news in English |
| mofa.gov.qa | Info on country, government, economy & tourism |

# Public Holidays & Annual Events

## Public Holidays

The two major public holidays in Qatar are religious ones: Eid Al Fitr and Eid Al Adha. Eid Al Fitr marks the end of the fasting month of Ramadan, which is the ninth month of the Islamic calendar (Hijri calendar). During this month, Muslims are required to abstain from food, drink, cigarettes and unclean thoughts from dawn until dusk. The Islamic calendar is based on the lunar months, so the beginning and the end of Ramadan is not fixed but it is decided instead on the sighting of the moon. As a result, religious holidays are only determined 24 hours in advance. Eid Al Fitr is usually marked by a three-day celebration and many businesses shut down during this time. Eid Al Adha, the festival of the sacrifice, commemorates Ibrahim's willingness to sacrifice his son to God. It follows Eid Al Fitr by around 70 days and is marked by a four-day celebration. There are two other important dates: Accession Day and National Day. Lailat Al Mi'raj celebrates the Prophet's ascension into heaven.

A relatively new holiday since 2012 is Qatar's annual National Sports Day, designed to promote healthy living. In 2015 it falls on 10 February and many businesses close for the day.

### Public Holidays 2014-2015

| | 2014 | 2015 |
|---|---|---|
| **Eid Al Fitr** (2-3 days; Moon) | July 28 | Jul 18 |
| **Eid Al Adha** (2-3 days; Moon) | Oct 4 | Sept 23 |
| **National Day** (Fixed) | Dec 18 | Dec 18 |
| **National Sports Day** | Feb 10 | Feb 10 |

Traditional Qatari dance

Essentials

Public Holidays & Annual Events

# Annual Events

### Commercial Bank Qatar Masters — January
Doha Golf Club — qatar-masters.com

The Qatar Masters is an annual event on the PGA European tour. The event attracts some of the world's best players who compete for a share of the $2.5 million prize money.

### Qatar ExxonMobil Open — January
Khalifa Int'l Tennis & Squash Complex — qatartennis.org

Doha's ATP men's tennis tournament attracts top names at the start of the sporting year each January; among recent winners are tennis ace Roger Federer (2011), France's Jo-Wilfried Tsonga (2012) and Richard Gasquet (2013) followed by Spain's Rafeal Nadal (2014).

### Qatar International Rally — January
Various Locations — qmmf.com

Taking place across Qatar's varied terrain, this three-day event starts and finishes on Doha Corniche. Spectate from various points along the route for a close-up of the action:

### Qatar Motor Show — February
Qatar National Convention Centre — qatarmotorshow.gov.qa

This is an annual draw for the motoring trade and consumers alike; in addition to showcasing the newest models by international automakers, the latest auto and performance trends are on display.

## Qatar International Equestrian Festival

February

Al Rayyan Racetrack

qrec.gov.qa

Some of the fastest horses in the world visit Doha for this festival held at Rayyan, in the north of the city.

## Qatar International Regatta

February

Doha Sailing Club

qatarsailing.org

A highly popular event with locals and expatriates, the Doha Sailing Club plays host to this celebration of all things boating every February.

## Qatar Ladies Open

February

Khalifa Int'l Tennis & Squash Complex

qatartennis.org

The best international players on the circuit will head to Qatar to compete for the Qatar Tennis Federation (QTF) cup.

## Halal Qatar Festival

March

Katara Cultural Village

katara.net

Launched in 2012, the week-and-a-half long event gives an insight into all things Halal, including the breeding of animals, animal trade and opportunities to sample some of Qatar's traditional foods.

## Powerboat Racing

March

The Corniche

f1h2o.com

Class 1 offshore powerboat racing is the fastest and most exhilarating of all watersports, and each year Qatar hosts two rounds of the world championship. Spectators can enjoy the action along Doha's Corniche and cheer on the local Qatar team which, despite being a relatively new entrant to the sport, has already posted some impressive results.

### Commercialbank Grand Prix Of Qatar — April
Losail International Circuit Lusail — motogp.com

The brand new Losail motor racing circuit outside Doha is the venue for the Qatar Commercialbank Grand Prix, a leg of the MotoGP World Championship. The circuit also hosts the Losail National Cup.

### Katara International Kites Family Day — May
Katara Cultural Village — katara.net

A public, family-friendly event with kite-building, flying and designing workshops, as well as entertainment from kite-flyers from around the world. Qatar held its first one at Katara Cultural Village in 2011.

### Eid Al Fitr — July (Moon)

Eid Al Fitr (the festival of the breaking of the fast) takes place at the end of the holy month of Ramadan. This occasion is often characterised by big family get-togethers and celebrations with feasts and gifts.

### Doha Film Festival — October
Various Locations — dohafilminstitute.com

This high-profile international movie festival, originally pioneered by Robert De Niro in New York, takes place annually in Doha. It brings together the top names in world cinema and is a must for film fans.

### Eid Al Adha  October (Moon)
Eid Al Adha (the festival of sacrifice, which marks the end of the pilgrimage to Mecca) takes place around October in 2014 and September in 2015 (depending on the sighting of the moon).

### National Day  18 December
This national celebration is a fairly recent addition to Qatar's public holidays and commemorates the assumption of power of Sheikh Jassem bin Mohamed bin Thani in 1868.

# Getting Around

**The car is king in Qatar, and a modern road network makes every corner of the country easy to reach.**

Qatar's excellent road network, and the minimal number of buses, trams and trains, means that getting from A to B is best done by car or taxi. Navigating your way around is easy; a series of north-south ring roads follow the shape of Doha's Corniche, while major routes head off north, south and west to link the capital with the rest of the country. Taxis are fairly easy to find, particularly around hotels and malls.

The bus system is relatively cheap for those who don't have a car. There is also a bus system that links many of Qatar's other cities with Doha. The warm weather and dubious driving can make it risky business for those who attempt to get around the city by bike. A metro is currently under construction in Doha, with the first phase scheduled for completion in 2018.

## Bicycle

While cycling the seven kilometres of the Corniche is popular, especially in the cooler months, there are no dedicated cycle tracks around the city. As a mode of transport to get you around the city, cycling is not a great choice. Thanks to the somewhat aggressive driving habits and heat, hopping on your bike to get to work is not an activity that is commonplace. However, there is a cycling federation, which organises regular rides and races for those who are keen to get pedalling; see qatarcf.org for more information.

# Boat

With so much coastline there is plenty for boat owners to see and do, but there are no regular passenger services linking coastal towns and cities. There was previously a ferry service between Iran and Qatar, operated by the Qatar National Navigation Company, but this has been halted indefinitely. However, it is possible to take a boat ride to some of the offshore islands or to cruise the bay aboard a traditional dhow. To organise one of these, your best bet is to contact one of the local tour operators or speak to your hotel concierge for private island tours.

# Bus

There is a public bus service throughout most neighbourhoods in Doha and to other major cities. The Al Ghanim Bus Station is located off of Grand Hamad Street in the middle of the city. The station is currently more of a depot for buses to come and go but this is made up for by the modern, clean, air-conditioned buses. The Karwa bus service is managed by Mowasalat.

Fares within the city range from about QR 3 to QR 9 depending on the distance travelled, and fares outside of town are usually very good value. Unlimited daily, weekly and monthly passes are available from the bus operator, Mowasalat, at the bus station. Otherwise you can pay the driver when you board (it is advisable to have the correct change). Further details on passes, saver cards and routes can be found on the Mowasalat website (mowasalat.com) or by calling 4458 8588.

# Driving & Car Hire

The country has a good network of roads and highways, generally in a decent state of repair and constantly being improved. Many of Doha's roundabouts, which were prone to confusing drivers, have mostly been replaced with signals. Signposts are almost always in English as well as Arabic. Petrol stations can be found throughout Doha and along the main roads in Qatar and most visitors will be pleasantly surprised to find the price of fuel is a lot lower than elsewhere in the world. This means that many motorists can afford to run gas-guzzling 4WDs, of which there are many on Qatar's roads.

If you intend to drive in Qatar you must have your wits about you and remain alert at all times, as speeding, tail-gating and sudden lane-changing are all too common. Be careful to contain your frustration though, as obscene gestures and examples of road-rage can result in severe penalties. Driving is on the right and seatbelts are mandatory for the driver and front seat passenger. A further hazard to be aware of when driving outside the towns is camels crossing the road.

In order to lease a car, you will need a credit card, a copy of your passport and a valid driving licence. There are a number of reputable leasing companies in Doha, many of which are internationally recognised. Some companies have branches at the airport. The longer the leasing period, the better the discount you will be given on the price. The monthly rate for leasing a car starts at QR 1,600 and QR 3,500 for a 4WD.

# Taxi

If you're planning to stay in Doha for a long visit, then relying on taxis may be a pain. At times it seems like there are not enough and, if you're unlucky, you may end up waiting a while for one. Over the last couple of years, the run-down orange-and-white taxis have slowly been replaced by the newer, and more expensive, blue cars. The new, blue Karwa taxi meters start at QR 4 and run at QR 1.20 per kilometre. Taxis that are picked up outside hotels will often charge a premium rate. To save yourself from the hassle of having to flag down a taxi, you can always order one in advance for an extra charge of QR 4 by calling 4458 8888. Taxi drivers know the city pretty well, although street

| Car Rental Agencies | |
|---|---|
| AAB Rent A Car | 4443 7000 |
| Al Muftah Rent A Car | 5589 1334 |
| Al Sulaiman Rent A Car | 4491 1711 |
| Almana Rent A Car – Hertz | 4448 9944 |
| Avis Qatar | 4462 2180 |
| Budget Rent A Car | 4431 0411 |
| Euro Dollar Rent A Car | 4432 1313 |
| Europcar | 4466 0677 |
| Mannai Autorent | 4448 3651 |
| Mustafawi Rent A Car | 4462 1542 |
| National Car Rental | 4436 6771 |
| Prestige Cars Co | 4420 9130 |
| Thrifty Car Rental | 4462 1180 |

names are not commonly used and most drivers navigate using the surrounding landmarks. The only taxis in service now at the international airport are the newer, blue taxis. Unlike the old orange taxis whose drivers would refuse to take you anywhere for less than QR 20 to QR 30, the new taxis have to use the meters. Just expect a higher pick-up charge from the airport.

## Walking

Perhaps because of the summer heat, or maybe because everybody can afford a luxury car, walking is not a common mode of transport in Qatar. Modern roads, ample parking and cars equipped with super-cool air-conditioning make driving a much more pleasant way to get around. However, there are plenty of areas suitable for those who walk for pleasure – the famous Corniche, which runs a 7km stretch from the Sheraton to Ras Abu Abboud, is always busy with active people striding, biking, rollerblading or pram-walking up and down.

### Further Out

To explore remote areas around Doha, you may want to hire a 4WD or join an organised tour. There are a few heritage sites, museums, forts and fishing villages around the country. Al Wakra, Umm Salal and Al Zubarah all have interesting sites that are worth visiting if you are in the area, but it is good to join organised tours as you may venture out only to find forts and towers are closed for renovation.

Essentials

**Essentials**

## Places To Stay

**Qatar's growing range of premium hotels provide a serving of glamour to visitors arriving in the region for business or pleasure.**

Qatar promotes itself as a high-quality destination, appealing to well-off tourists, business travellers and the lucrative MICE market. Luxury five-star hotels dominate the accommodation options, although there are also a number of reasonably priced hotels out there. Another alternative is to book into a serviced hotel apartment, which tends to work out cheaper than hotels for longer stays. Since its successful bid to host the 2022 Football World Cup, Qatar has outlined significant investment plans for tourism infrastructure.

Occupancy rates in Doha's hotels have been high in recent years thanks to the fact that visitor numbers have increased faster than new hotels have opened up. However, thousands of hotel rooms have been added in the past few years, with plans for the total number to reach 30,000 by the end of 2014. Most five-star hotels are located in the West Bay area, which, unsurprisingly, is also home to most of the country's beaches. More expensive hotels usually provide direct access to the beach, and most also boast a luxurious spa and a collection of restaurants. Among the latest additions to the luxury hotel scene are the St Regis Hotel (stregisdoha.com) and a collection of cosy boutique hotels in Souk Waqif (swbh.com).

**HILTON HHONORS**

## LOCATED HERE
## STRICTLY FOR SELFISH REASONS.

Located in the bustling West Bay Area, Hilton Doha is the perfect combination of business and leisure.
Hilton Doha offers 309 rooms with uninterrupted views over the Arabian Gulf, a private beach, a pool and the choice of 6 different dining destination including the famous Trader Vic's.

For room reservations please visit doha.hilton.com or call +974-4423-3333

**Hilton**
DOHA

West Bay | Diplomatic District Street | Doha | Qatar

## Places To Stay | Essentials

### Concorde Hotel
concordedoha.com
4407 3333
This popular hotel is conveniently located just a short drive from the airport. Facilities include a state-of-the-art gym, massage room and swimming pool. Be sure to try the elegant Italian restaurant Trattoria.  **Map** 1 J5

### Courtyard By Marriott
marriott.com
4419 5555
Situated within West Bay, the hotel is ideally located for business guests, while the adjoining mall offers ample retail therapy right on their doorstep. The hotel also connects with the newly opened Renaissance hotel.  **Map** 1 G1

### Grand Heritage Hotel
grandheritagedoha.com
4445 5555
This luxurious hotel and spa boasts 133 beautiful rooms as well as four suites. Guests enjoy access to an indoor lap pool and gym. There's also an authentic tea lounge, and a lovely Mediterranean restaurant on site.  **Map** 3 A5

فندق كونكورد

# CONCORDE
HOTEL

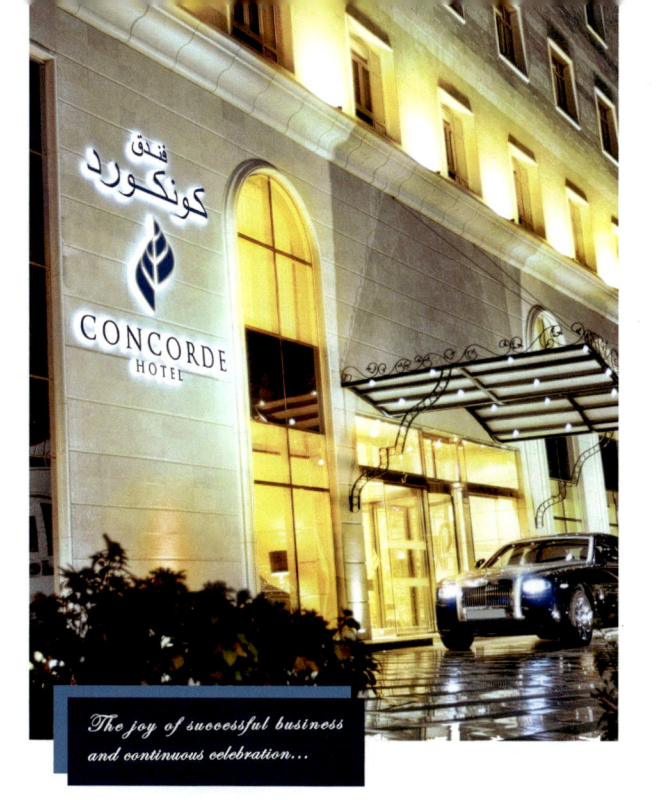

*The joy of successful business and continuous celebration...*

**CONCORDE HOTEL DOHA**
Tel : +974 4407 3333
Email : info@concordedoha.com
www.concordedoha.com
AIRPORT ROAD, P.O.BOX 200000
DOHA, STATE OF QATAR

## Places To Stay

### Doha Marriott Hotel
marriott-doha.com
4429 8888
Located a few minutes from the airport, this modern hotel is favoured by business travellers as it provides a wide range of facilities. Its restaurants are popular and the view from the rooftop is worth seeing.  **Map** 1 K4

### Grand Hyatt
doha.grand.hyatt.com
4448 1234
To say that this hotel is grand is an understatement – the giant crystal chandelier in the lobby sets the tone of things to come. Most rooms have sea views and there's a 400 metre private beach to enjoy.  **Map** 3 D1

### Hilton Doha
hilton.com
4423 3333
Hilton Doha boasts a scenic location in the Diplomatic Area. The rooms offer sweeping views of the Arabian Gulf and there are many eating and entertainment options, as well as a business centre.  **Map** 1 H1

### InterContinental Doha
intercontinental.com/doha
4484 4444
This five-star hotel has Doha's longest stretch of private beach and largest free-form pool. It also boasts a brilliant range of dining and nightlife facilities, from Greek restaurant Mykonos to trendy bar Lava Lounge. **Map** 3 D2

### InterContinental Doha The CIty
intercontinental.com/dohathecity
4015 8888
This West Bay hotel is located close to the area's many attractions. In-house, you'll find some excellent dining and nightlife options as well as a good health and wellness club. **Map** 1 G1

### K108 Hotel
k108hotel.com
4433 3000
This chic boutique hotel has a central location and modern, stylish rooms. It's within walking distance of Souk Waqif and the Museum of Islamic Arts. Plus, the hotel donates its profits to charities and other important causes. **Map** 1 J5

**Essentials**

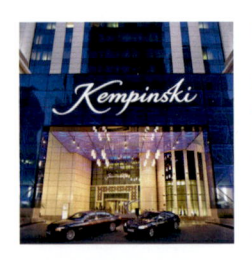

### Kempinski Residences & Suites, Doha
kempinski.com/doha
4405 3333
Towering above Doha's business district, this popular hotel features spacious rooms and residences, a Pure Leisure and Wellness Centre, and some great restaurants. **Map** 1 H1

### La Cigale Hotel
lacigalehotel.com
4428 8888
A short ride from the airport, La Cigale Hotel features exclusive amenities. The new hotel has a reputation for first-class hospitality. It has five restaurants, including live cooking stations at Le Cigalon. **Map** 1 F5

### Oryx Rotana
rotana.com
4402 3333
Close to Doha International Airport, this hotel is an affordable, five-star retreat for business travellers. The 400 room hotel has access to an outdoor pool, fitness centre and spa.
**Map** 1 K6

### The Ritz-Carlton Doha
ritzcarlton.com
4484 8000
The Ritz features exquisitely decorated rooms with breathtaking views. You can enjoy watersports and a good mix of spa treatments at this hotel, and the restaurants serve international and Arabic cuisine.  **Map** 3 D1

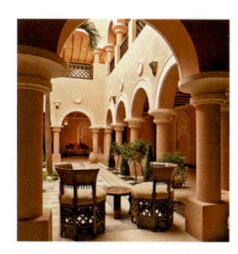

### Sharq Village & Spa
sharqvillage.com
4425 6666
Sharq Village & Spa is reminiscent of a traditional Qatari village, but with all the modern-day elegance and facilities. On site are the flagship Six Senses Spa and Al Dana restaurant along the beach.  **Map** 1 K5

### Sheraton Doha Resort & Convention Hotel
sheratondoha.com
4485 4444
Currently under renovation, this stunning pyramid landmark situated on acres of landscaped gardens overlooks West Bay, close to Doha's busy city centre.  **Map** 1 H2

**Essentials**

## Essentials — Places To Stay

### Somerset West Bay
somerset.com
4420 3333
Located in the Diplomatic Area, this hotel is convenient for those here on business, and its kitted-out serviced apartments offer views of the Arabian Gulf. Facilities include a swimming pool, sauna and gym. **Map** 1 H1

### St Regis Doha
stregisdoha.com
4446 0000
This new luxury option right on the beach has 336 rooms and suites offering stunning views – some of them even have private terraces. It's located conveniently close to Katara Cultural Village. **Map** 3 D2

### Zubarah Boutique Hotel
zubarahhotels.com
4447 0000
A thoroughly modern and stylish hotel with just 45 rooms and suites. This dry establishment has a very family-friendly atmosphere and boasts a lovely restaurant, charming cafe and an enticing spa. **Map** 1 G6

# ST. REGIS

DOCHA

## ONE ADDRESS, MANY MAGNIFICENT EXPERIENCES

*Welcome to The St. Regis Doha, the finest address in Qatar. Overlooking the beautiful Arabian Gulf, the hotel is a fusion of Middle Eastern splendour and traditional St. Regis hospitality. It presents 336 guest rooms and 58 captivating suites with Butler Service. The hotel also features 11 signature restaurants & lounges, a world class Remède Spa and an Olympic-size pool with private cabanas and an exclusive beach.*

AL GASSAR RESORT
AT WEST BAY
STREGISDOHA.COM
974.4446.0000

A LEGACY OF LUXURY,
NOW AT OVER 30 OF THE WORLD'S
FINEST HOTELS & RESORTS

AFRICA   THE AMERICAS   ASIA
EUROPE   THE MIDDLE EAST

STREGIS.COM

spg
Starwood
Preferred
Guest

©2010–2013 Starwood Hotels & Resorts Worldwide, Inc. All Rights Reserved. Preferred Guest, SPG, St. Regis and their logos are the trademarks of Starwood Hotels & Resorts Worldwide, Inc., or its affiliates.

## Hotel Apartments

The cost of renting a furnished hotel apartment is cheaper in the long term than a standard hotel room. The daily rate for a one-bed apartment is around QR 1,000, while the monthly rate for a two-bed should be between QR 12,000 and QR 14,000. For a more luxurious option, try the serviced apartments at the Ascott Doha (4497 1111).

## Campsites

Camping is not a regulated activity in Qatar and as such there are no official campsites with facilities. However, camping takes place on a regular basis by residents and locals and is certainly a part of local tradition. For expatriates living in Qatar, it is perhaps best to take a cautionary approach unless invited camping by a local. A number of local tour operators provide organised camping trips that include meals and entertainment among the sand dunes.

| 3* and 4* Hotels | | |
|---|---|---|
| Al Bustan Hotel | Al Slata | 4432 888 |
| Century Hotel | Umm Ghuwailina | 4445 5111 |
| Le Park Hotel | Al Sadd | 4432 2212 |
| Mercure Grand Hotel Doha City Centre | Al Jasra | 4446 2222 |
| Mövenpick Hotel Doha | Al Salata | 4429 1111 |
| Radisson Blu | Al Muntazah | 2448 7777 |
| Safir Doha Hotel | Najma | 4445 3333 |
| Swiss-Belhotel Doha | Al Mirqab | 4407 8888 |

## Luxurious living in the Heart of Doha

Located at the north end of Corniche Bay, offering picturesque views of the Arabian Gulf and within walking distance to Qatar's best known retail and entertainment destinations. Make yourself at home at the prestigious Ascott Doha. **Because life is about living**

### ASCOTT
DOHA

Enjoy Ascott's Best Rate Guarantee | www.the-ascott.com | +973 4497 1111

*Ascott Doha* is managed by The Ascott Limited, a member of CapitaLand. It is the largest international serviced residence owner-operator with more than 200 properties in over 80 cities across Asia Pacific, Europe and the Gulf region. It operates three award-winning brands *Ascott*, *Citadines* and *Somerset*.

# Exploring

| | |
|---|---|
| **Explore Qatar** | 70 |
| **Al Sadd & Al Rayyan Road** | 72 |
| **Al Dafna & West Bay** | 76 |
| **Doha Corniche** | 82 |
| **Khalifa Street & Al Luqta Street** | 88 |
| **Salwa Road & Al Aziziya** | 92 |
| **Souk Area & Souk Waqif** | 98 |
| **Outside Of Doha** | 104 |
| **Tours & Sightseeing** | 110 |

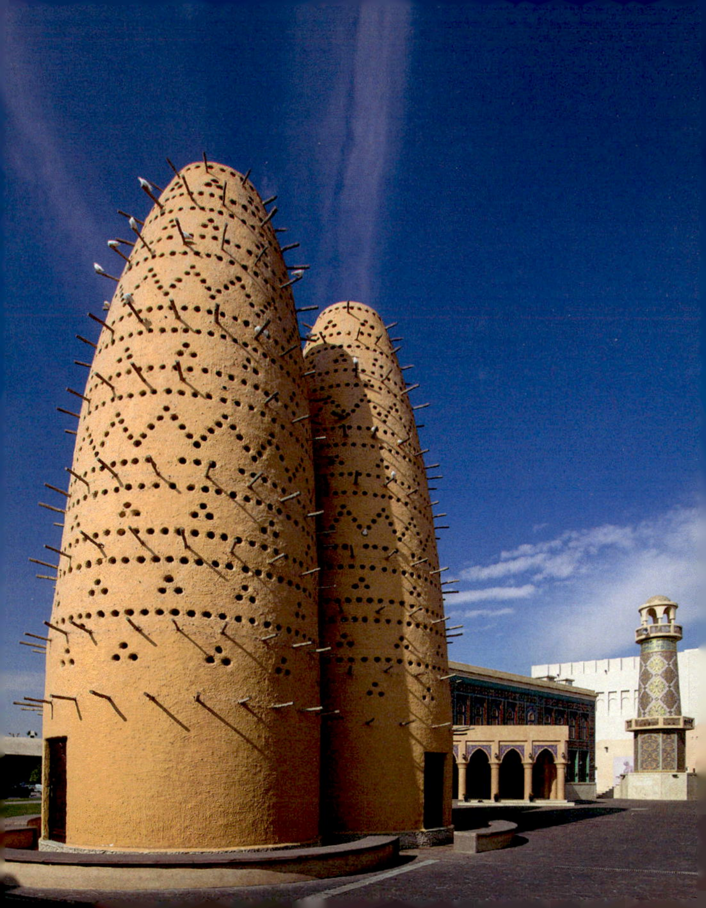

# Explore Qatar

**In its bid to become the cultural capital of the Middle East, Qatar boasts plenty of attractions to explore.**

Qatar's bizarre mix of barren desert, expansive coast, and booming urban sprawl makes for an exciting place to investigate. For the historically oriented traveller, archaeological sites abound both in and out of the capital, Doha, and the government has taken great care in preserving the country's surprisingly detailed past. Art and architecture buffs are equally catered for – the Museum of Islamic Art is the premiere cultural destination in the region, and the ever-ascending skyscrapers in the Al Dafna District wouldn't seem out of place in a science fiction novel.

The vast majority of Qatar's population lives in Doha and most of the country's attractions are there as well. The city revolves around the Corniche-lined bay. At the south end of the bay lies Doha International Airport. Working north around the bay, you'll find the souk area, which includes the accurately restored Souk Waqif. Follow the Corniche even further and you'll soon find yourself among the towering skyscrapers of the West Bay area. The Corniche itself is a major attraction and a walk along it, if the climate's right, is a must for any visitor.

Travelling south-west from the souks you'll run into the shop-lined Salwa Road before reaching the Villaggio Mall, Aspire Park and Education City.

*Mosque and reflecting pool*

To finish the loop, drive east on Al Luqta Street and Khalifa Street to witness another of the city's main thoroughfares. This corridor will take you back to the Corniche, where you'll be greeted by the skyscrapers of the Al Dafna District.

Just before you reach the Corniche, head north along Al Istiqlal Road and within 10 minutes you will arrive at one of Doha's latest evening hotspots. The Cultural Village of Katara offers the city's only public beach access while, at night, the area comes alive with outdoor music from the many shisha cafes along the pedestrian-only pathways.

Travelling further north and you'll find Doha's most luxurious destination – The Pearl, where a stunning marina, boutique stores and fine-dining restaurants await you at the newly dubbed 'Italian Riviera of the Middle East.'

**Exploring**

**Exploring**

# Al Sadd & Al Rayyan Road

**Travelling through old Qatar, Al Rayyan Road and its surrounding areas are a visual treat for visitors.**

Named after the suburb to which it leads, Al Rayyan Road has long been a main artery through Doha. The roundabout-laden thoroughfare starts at the east end of the city, near the souks, and travels west past the new Medical City and Education City. Al Sadd Street, which runs parallel to Al Rayyan Road, is a busy commercial area with restaurants and shops, including the Royal Plaza shopping mall. Running between Al Rayyan and Al Sadd is Jawaan Street, which has the Grand Regency and Millennium hotels as well as Al Asmakh mall. For restaurants and nightlife establishments in the area, see Venue Finder.

## Al Wajbah Fort
Nr Emir's Palace, Al Rayyan

With its high towers and thick walls, this fort is considered one of the oldest in the country. It was the site of a famous battle in 1893, when the people of Qatar defeated the Ottoman forces. As a result, the name of Al Wajbah evokes a strong feeling of pride among local people. To reach the fort, turn off the roundabout before the Emir's palace (if driving from Doha), go over the speed bumps and turn right at the end of the gravel track.

Al Wajbah Fort

### Fun City
4428 9250
Centrepoint, Al Sadd
This small but nicely maintained soft play area has a separate section with dressing-up clothes, slides and a drawing table. You pay per hour for the play areas and the small rides cost extra. There's also a kids' hairdressers upstairs. Parents suffer, though, because there are only three chairs.  **Map** 1 E5

### Ray's Reef
4413 0000
Royal Plaza, Al Sadd
royalplazadoha.com
This new play place has a bright nautical theme and a small cafe. It has two adventure play areas with tunnels, slides and cannons for firing balls from the ball pool. There's also a home corner and a TV area with plush red velvet step seating. Creative kids can make use of the easels and paints. For a fixed price, children can play with what they like, but the many arcade games cost extra.  **Map** 1 E5

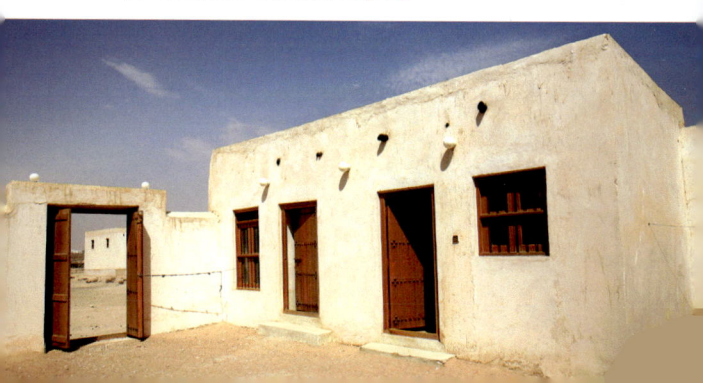

Exploring

Exploring

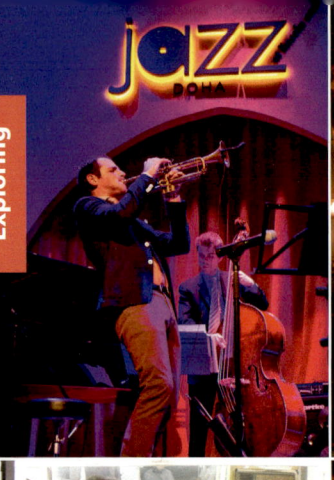

jazz
DOHA

SALOON

# If you only do one thing in...
# Al Sadd & Al Rayyan Road

Experience 'old Qatar' and admire the traditional architecture while driving along Al Rayyan Road, before dining in one of its many traditional restaurants or street cafes.

## Best for...

**Culture:** Al Wajbah Fort is one of the oldest in the country and a piece of heritage that the locals are very proud of.

**Eating:** It's not pretty, but if you're new to the Middle East, you can't leave without tasting an authentic shawarma from Automatic.

**Families:** Take the kids to Ray's Reef. They can let loose in the adventure play areas while you relax at the cafe.

**Sightseeing:** Starting near the souks, Al Rayyan Road is long and well worth a drive. The ageing buildings deserve a snapshot or two.

*Clockwise from top left: Jazz At The Lincoln, authentic shawarma, ornate chest and a barbershop*

**Exploring**

# Al Dafna & West Bay

## Once a Doha backwater, the northern part of the city has come to define the entire country's fast-paced development.

Cranes, freshly paved roads and futuristic skyscrapers announce your arrival into the Al Dafna and West Bay area of Doha. What was once a distant outcrop of the main city, this tiny peninsula on the north side of the bay has become the centre of Doha's incredible and increasingly rapid development. Several top hotels are located here, as well as City Center Doha, one of the country's most famous shopping malls. Further north lies West Bay, home to The Pearl and the newly completed Cultural Village of Katara, which occupies a huge open-air amphitheatre, outdoor restaurants and shisha cafes, as well as art galleries and performing art spaces. For restaurants and nightlife establishments in the area, see **Venue Finder**.

### I-Net Cafe                                4493 3312
*City Center Doha, Al Dafna*

A dark and noisy den for teenage gaming fans, I-Net offers network gaming and internet access for all ages. Enthusiasts can play each other or go online. Despite being called a cafe it offers no refreshments, so you'll have to tear yourself away from the games to grab a drink elsewhere. There are no arcade games or other attractions here, but it should keep gaming fanatics happy for hours. **Map** 1 H1

*Qatar Financial Centre*

Exploring

Al Dafna & West Bay

## Katara Cultural Village

Off Lusail St, Al Gassar  katara.net

Since this stunning venue first opened in 2010, Katara Cultural Village has remained a favourite leisure destination with residents and visitors, both during the day and in the evening. As a night-time hub, the village encompasses an open-air amphitheatre, opera house, drama theatre, a handicraft souk, as well as a good selection of restaurants and cafes that include Shawarma Albisana for some authentic Middle Eastern bites. During the day, the public beach is a main attraction with plenty of activities in the water for children, and watersports activities are available for the young at heart. The private beach entry is QR 100 for adults and kids are free.  **Map** 3 D2

## The Pearl

Al Gassar  thepearlqatar.com

This is Qatar's largest foray into the man-made island trend that has come to define many cities in the Gulf. With an extraordinary collection of high-end designer retailers and boutique shops, The Pearl is worth a visit to simply surround yourself with luxury. Branches of enviable brands such as Hermes, Armani, Kenzo, MaxMara, Jimmy Choo, Vera Wang, Chloe, Missoni, Roberto Cavalli and Alexander McQueen offer fresh off-the-catwalk haute couture, handbags, jewellery and fashion accessories. If your Louboutins need a rest, you can stop for a break at world-famous, Alison Nelson's Chocolate Bar, or sip an espresso on the boardwalk while watching extravagant yachts sail by.  **Map** 3 D2

Exploring

Al Dafna & West Bay

Exploring

## If you only do one thing in...
# Al Dafna & West Bay

Take a stroll around Porto Arabia at The Pearl Qatar before jumping on a speed boat with Ronautica and enjoy the view of the coast from the sea.

## Best for...

**Eating:** Katara Cultural Village has plenty of mouthwatering eateries to choose from; try Shawarma Albisana for an introduction to Middle Eastern culinary delights.

**Families:** Take the kids ice skating at City Center Doha.

**Outdoor:** Relax at Doha's popular private beach at the Katara Cultural Village where swimming, inflatables and watersports abound.

**Nightlife:** Watch a show at the stunning open air amphitheatre at the Katara Cultural Village; previous acts have included renowned Lebanese singer Magida El Roumi.

*Clockwise from top left: Ongoing construction, Doha City Center Mall, Qatar financial district*

**Exploring**

## Doha Corniche

**The heart of the city, Doha's perfectly manicured Corniche was purpose-built for late-night strolls and peaceful people watching.**

Doha revolves around its gorgeously landscaped Corniche. Running along the length of the bay, the road starts at the impressive Sharq Village & Spa in the south and ends up at the Sheraton Doha in the northern Al Dafna area. Several of the country's top museums line the curving boulevard, including the iconic Museum of Islamic Art, which has become a cultural beacon in the region. One of the Corniche's greatest assets is its walkability. In a city consisting mainly of highways, the tree-lined path along the sea presents a perfect opportunity for experiencing a city that is usually seen through a windscreen. For restaurants and nightlife establishments in the area, see Venue Finder.

### Museum Of Islamic Art
The Corniche, Al Souq

4422 4444
mia.org.qa

Architect IM Pei has created an elegant home for this impressive collection. The building is subtle yet beautiful, with details drawn from a wide range of Islamic influences. The collection is showcased as a journey through time, countries and cultures, and the oldest piece dates from the ninth century. Along with the permanent and temporary galleries, there is a library, an auditorium and the outside park has also become popular in its own right.  **Map** 1 H4

Exploring

Doha Corniche

### Museum Park
**Nr Qatar National Museum**
Next to the currently closed Qatar National Museum, and overlooking the Corniche, this large grassy area stretches for quite a distance. It has lots of play equipment and a big paved area, which is great for cycling and skateboarding. There is plenty of space for running around and enjoying picnics. There aren't many trees, however, so the park is more enjoyable in the evenings and during the cooler winter months. **Map** 1 J4

### National Museum of Qatar
4452 5555
**Museum Park St, Al Salata**
qma.com.qa
Due to a fire, the museum has been under renovation and is scheduled to reopen in 2016. It showcases various coins, jewellery, traditional clothing, household items and tools. There are areas that recreate Bedouin scenes, as well as an exhibit on the oil industry. For updates on the reopening, it is recommended that you call the Ministry of Culture, Arts & Heritage on 4402 2222. **Map** 1 J4

### Rumeilah Park (Al Bidda Park)
**The Corniche, Al Rumeilah**
Located opposite the Corniche, this beautifully landscaped park tends to be busiest on Fridays and in the evenings. It has an amphitheatre and an area called the Heritage Village, that was built to resemble a traditional village. There are a few shops that open sporadically, and well-maintained toilets. A gallery, displaying work by local artists, is open 9am to 12pm and 4pm to 9pm. **Map** 1 F3

Exploring

Doha Corniche

askexplorer.com

85

**Exploring**

# If you only do one thing in...
# Doha Corniche

Head straight to the Museum of Islamic Art. The perfectly executed museum is already being hailed as the best cultural attraction in the region.

## Best for...

**Eating:** Go to the promenade and opt for a table at Al Mourjan, where you can dine on some of the tastiest Lebanese dishes in Doha.

**Families:** If the weather's right, spend a day at Rumeilah Park and let the kids wander while you enjoy the bay breeze.

**Outdoor:** A trip to Doha isn't complete without a stroll along the well-groomed, tree-lined Corniche – a waterfront promenade that's also popular with joggers in the morning.

**Sightseeing:** The section of the Corniche in front of the Ministry of Interior provides the most interesting photo opportunities of the rising skyline.

*Top: Marina in Doha; Bottom: Qatar National Museum*

# Khalifa Street & Al Luqta Street

**Running directly into the cleverly designed Education City, this main corridor eventually cuts through the country to the west coast.**

Beginning at the Oryx Roundabout near the Corniche, Khalifa Street runs directly west out of the city and eventually turns into Al Luqta Street. Inside Doha proper, the corridor is home to Al Jazeera and Qatar TV, but things don't start to get interesting until the city starts to thin out, giving way to the interesting Education City, Al Shaqab stud farm and eventually the Sheikh Faisal Bin Qassim Al Thani Museum.

### Al Shaqab
Nr Education City, Al Shaqub

4454 6320
alshaqab.com

Owned by Sheikh Hamad bin Khalifa Al Thani, this farm provides the opportunity for viewing gorgeous thoroughbred Arabian horses, many of which are world champions. Visits by appointment only for individuals or groups can be made directly with the farm. Al Shaqab's tours aim to raise awareness about equestrian culture, and can be specially designed to be educational, informative or more recreational.
**Map** 3 A4

### Dahl Al Hamam Park
Nr Al Markhiya & Arab League Sts, Dahl Al Hamam
Located on the corner of Arab League Street and Al Markiyah Street, this sizeable park has lots of grass and an enormous

paved area. There is a cafe selling snacks and drinks that opens after 5pm. The families-only park opens from 2pm until 11pm, so you can picnic and play until well after bedtime.
**Map** 1 C1

### Education City
Al Luqta Street                                        qf.org.qa

Driving into Education City from the relatively barren area surrounding it is a somewhat surreal experience. Windblown desert speckled with box-shaped buildings immediately transforms into lush lawns lined with some of the most contemporary architecture in the Middle East. The massive complex is a cornerstone of the Qatar Foundation's master plan and some of the best universities are represented here, including Cornell and Georgetown. **Map** 3 A4

### Mathaf Arab Museum Of Modern Art    4402 8855
Off Al Luqta St, Education City                mathaf.org.qa

Since December 2010, modern Arab art has had this massive 5,500 sq. metres of display space to call home. Located in a converted school building in Education City, the works on display span from 1849 to the present and every Arab country is represented. Mathaf aims to foster communication within the art community and the community at large. Hands-on workshops and curatorial tours aid this end. The library, Maktaba, is stocked for both academic and casual users. Should you wish to pick up a memento, a small gift shop is located near the exit. Free admission. Open 11am-6pm. Friday 3pm-8pm. Mondays closed. **Map** 3 A4

**Exploring**

## If you only do one thing in...
# Khalifa Street & Al Luqta Street

Take in some of the most impressive works of art at the Arab Museum Of Modern Art, before sidestepping into their arty cafe with coffee, cake and an art book.

## Best for...
**Families:** Call ahead and take your kids to see the beautiful Arabian horses at Al Shaqab Stud, and leave time for the new visitor centre and museum.

**Outdoor:** Despite only being open to families, Dahal Al Hamam Park is one of the nicest in the city and has a large outdoor play area.

**Sightseeing:** Although you can't take a tour without knowing someone on the inside, it's worth driving past the Al Jazeera headquarters on Khalifa Street just to see the hub of Arab media.

**Exploring**

# Salwa Road & Al Aziziya

## Whether you're looking for energetic nightlife or a fun place to take the family, Salwa Road fits the bill.

Starting at Doha's unofficial nightlife hub, the Radisson Blu, Salwa is another of Doha's main arteries. Several of the city's most popular restaurants line the wide street, as do many of the old souks, including the animal and vegetable markets. Drive far enough and you'll no doubt run into the Aspire complex. Directly after the Fish Market sits the area of Al Aziziya, which is home to the Villaggio Mall. For restaurants and nightlife establishments in the area, see Venue Finder.

### Al Muntazah Park
#### C Ring Road
This is one of the older parks in Doha, with large grassy areas and mature trees. Located at the corner of the C Ring Road and Al Muntazah Street, the park is only accessible to women and children (boys up to the age of nine) and tends to be busiest in the evenings and at the end of the week. Entrance is free of charge. **Map** 1 G6

### Animal Market
#### Wholesale Market St, Abu Hamour
This is one of the few places in Qatar that will truly make you feel like an outsider. Western visitors are rare, but the vendors are friendly and eager to talk to you, although their English

is often very basic. In case you are interested, a young camel will set you back around QR 5,000, and you can get an adult one for QR 10,000 upwards. Sheep and goats go for about QR 500 each and if you pay a bit extra the sellers will prepare the animal for eating.  **Map** 3 B6

### Aspire Academy For Sports Excellence   4413 6570
Nr Villaggio Mall, Baaya     aspire.qa

The first-class facilities at this sports academy include the world's largest purpose-built indoor sports dome, seven outdoor football pitches, an Olympic-size swimming pool, and specially designed fitness rooms. This is in addition to a dedicated medical centre and lecture halls for over 1,000 students. Aspire is also actively involved in the local community, and many schools have fitness classes with Aspire staff. The centre's facilities are open to the public via the Aspire Active classes (4413 6219). There are separate classes for men, women and different ages of children, in a variety of sports and fitness disciplines, making the aspire academy a great destinatin for a family day out. Some of the adult classes include spinning, cardio workouts and yoga, with kickboxing, boxing, and circuits for the men and Pilates, pre and post-natal classes, BeautyFull weight loss, dance cardio and aquatics for the girls. There is also a range of classes for mothers and babies, toddlers and young children. Aspire organises programmes for those with diabetes, with a specialist weight camp to help children avoid obesity. The classes are always well attended.  **Map** 3 A5

### Aspire Park

**Nr Villaggio Mall, Baaya**

Doha's largest park covers no less than 88 hectares (the size of more than 80 football pitches). The varied attractions include a large lake, jogging track, outdoor gym stations, shaded seating areas and a restaurant. Although more than 700 trees have been planted to create stunning greenery, there is not an overabundance of shade; those looking to bask in the sunshine will find plenty of open areas too. The park is also open in the evening for casual strolls. **Map** 3 A5

### Fish Market

**Salwa Rd, Abu Hamour**

This is not a place for those with weak stomachs; the odour is quite intense, but think of it as a cultural adventure. The air-conditioned market opens at 04:00 and the early morning is the best time for photographs since the fish bins are usually full and local restaurant buyers are abundant. Most of the vendors speak limited English, but are happy to try to explain the catch of the day. Well worth a visit if you like witnessing more 'authentic' ways of life. **Map** 3 B6

### Gondolania Theme Park

**Villaggio Mall, Baaya**

4403 9888
gondolania.com

This exotically named entertainment centre is located near Villaggio Mall. There is a bowling centre, a go kart track, video games and a range of exciting attractions including a rollercoaster, boat ride, Ferris wheel, carousel, bumper cars and more. **Map** 3 A5

### Jungle Zone

4499 9699
hyattplaza.com

Hyatt Plaza, Baaya

This children's area has nine attractions that are all themed around the jungle world. It is located in the foodcourt so parents can eat and let the children play all in one spot. Prices are QR 55 at weekends (Thursday to Saturday) and QR 40 during the week. **Map** 3 A5

### National Heritage Library

Nr Ras Abu Abboud & Jabir Bin Mohd Sts, Al Rufaa

This collection of 100,000 books, manuscripts, maps and scientific instruments are housed in a large villa on a quiet side street. One of the highlights is a rare set of volumes detailing Napoleon's expedition to Egypt in 1798. They are happy to give tours if you call in advance. **Map** 1 J5

**Exploring**

Exploring

محلات العائلات
FAMILY SHOP

# If you only do one thing in...
# Salwa Road & Al Aziziya

Bargain for a baby goat at the Animal Souk. Visitors are rare here so you'll see an untainted view of old Doha.

## Best for...

**Culture:** If the Animal Souk isn't culturally 'intense' enough for you, head to the fish market.

**Eating:** For some of the best Lebanese food in town, pop over to Layali Restaurant; the hummus is not to be missed.

**Families:** Aspire Park is perfect for a relaxing family day outdoors.

**Sightseeing:** Drive through Aspire Academy to get a glimpse of Khalifa Stadium and the landmark Aspire Tower, now the Torch Hotel.

Clockwise from top left: Decorative shop sign near Salwa Road, the Fish Market, Aspire Academy

# Souk Area & Souk Waqif

**The cultural capital of Qatar, Souk Waqif's stone walls and cobbled alleyways house some of Doha's best-kept secrets.**

Doha's souk area has long been the centre of activity for the country. Rural Bedouins used to travel to the market to sell their milk, meat and crafts. The city's oldest market, Souk Waqif, was renovated in 2004 using traditional building methods and materials. The resulting complex is now one of the most beautiful and authentic modern souks in the Gulf. The most refreshing aspect of the souk area is its dual purpose – tourists can easily stroll the narrow alleys in search of souvenirs while locals can purchase everything from fishing nets to pots and pans. In short, this is one attraction no visit to Qatar is complete without. For restaurants and nightlife establishments in the area, see the Venue Finder.

### Doha Fort (Al Koot Fort Museum)
Jassim Bin Mohammed St, Al Bidda      qma.com.qa

This white Moorish-style fort, next to Souk Waqif, has recently been restored and is open to the public for free. Located on the corner of Jasim bin Mohammed and Al Qalaa streets, it was built in 1927 to protect the souk from thieves. It is one of the few remaining military forts in Doha. One of the more fascinating features of the structure is the roofless, wall-less mosque that sits in the courtyard. **Map** 1 H4

Souk Waqif Art Centre

Souk Area & Souk Waqif

Exploring

askexplorer.com

99

### Orientalist Museum

Off Al Muthaf St, Salata qma.com.qa

This small white building is home to an impressive collection of Orientalist paintings and drawings, showing life in the Arab world in the 19th century. The paintings were collected by Sheikh Hassan bin Mohammed Al Thani over 15 years, and he donated them in 2005. To view the paintings, you need to make an appointment to be shown around by Fathi Hamzaoui, who talks you through the major artists and their work (his English is reasonable, but he prefers to speak in French or Arabic). **Map** 1 J4

### Al Markhiya Gallery

4442 8007

Souk Waqif, Al Jasra almarkhiyagallery.com

This small but esteemed gallery is located in the middle of the Souk Waqif. Al Markhiya's mission is to promote regional art, whether that be painting, sculpture or photography, by networking with international galleries. Paintings by new and established artists are featured here. **Map** 1 H4

### Windtower House

Off Grand Hamad & Ali bin Abdulla Sts, Al Jasra

The Windtower House is notable for being one of the last traditional windtowers in Qatar. You will find it off Grand Hamad Street and Ali bin Abdullah Street, enclosed within the downmarket Najada Shopping Plaza. Windtowers, known as barjeel in Arabic, were used in the days before electricity as a primitive form of air conditioning. They work by drawing fresh cool air into a house. **Map** 1 H5

Souk Area & Souk Waqif

Exploring

Exploring

# If you only do one thing in...
# Souk Area & Souk Waqif

Just walk. Souk Waqif's renovation was so well-executed that it warrants at least a day of wandering through its beautiful maze of alleyways.

## Best for...

**Culture:** Al Markhiya Gallery showcases art from across the Arab world in a variety of formats including paintings, textiles, and clay sculptures.

**Eating:** Book a teppanyaki table at Asia Live! and marvel at the culinary entertainment.

**Families:** Walk the kids to Doha Fort and let them imagine the history that took place there.

**Outdoor:** Head to the upstairs terrace at Tajine to sample some subtle Moroccan flavours, while enjoying the cool bay breeze.

# Outside of Doha

**Amateur archaeologists will love exploring the barren expanses and fort-littered coasts. Rent a car, bring a map and enjoy the solitude.**

Although the majority of Qatar's attractions are located in and around Doha, a trip through the desert allows visitors a chance to see a more traditional side of the country. The north-west coast is littered with old fortifications and empty stone houses. Places like Al Zubarah are filled with remnants of 'old Qatar', including the Zubarah Fort. It's also worth taking a trip into the desert, especially if you're heading to the Inland Sea in the south of the peninsula. If vacant beaches are your thing, head west towards Ras Abrouq, just north of Dukhan, which offers great, empty sandy beaches.

## Al Jassasiya Carvings
### 60km North of Doha, Nr Huwailah & Fuwairat

These rocky hills that overlook the north-eastern coast of Qatar, between the two villages of Al Huwailah and Fuwairit, contain more than 900 prehistoric carvings depicting different types of boats. The carvings also show rows of cup marks or depressions, believed by some to have been used for traditional games called al aailah and al haloosah. Others believe that the depressions were designed simply to catch rain water. A must-visit for history buffs, be warned that the area is difficult to find, so you may want to arrange a trip through a tour company.

*Inside the fort tower at Umm Salal Mohammed*

## Al Khor Museum

4472 1866

Al Khor Corniche, North of Doha

The rooms on the ground floor of Al Khor Museum showcase the fishing, pearling and dhow building industries, while the upper floor displays archaeological finds from the neolithic and bronze ages. There's a shaded area next to the museum with a playground and views of the harbour and sea. After visiting the museum, drive further along the Corniche and visit the old watchtowers that still stand guard over the town.

## Al Rakiyat Fort

Northwest of Doha   qma.com.qa

This fort was built between the 17th and 19th centuries, and restored in 1988. It is made of stone and mud and, similar

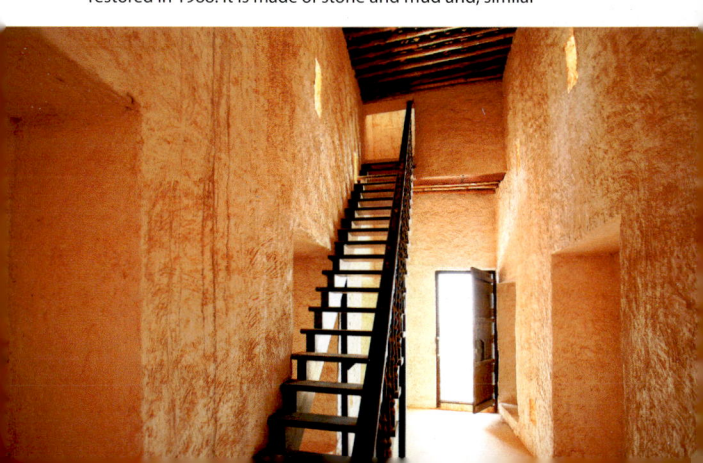

Exploring

to other forts in the country, is rectangular with a tower at each corner. The fort is located near a camel farm, just off the coastal road between Al Zubarah and Madinat Al Shamal. You'll have to drive off-road for a few hundred metres but it is possible in a normal car. The site is open to the public, but apart from the building itself there's little else to see.

## Zubarah
### Northern Qatar

Visit the remains of this important 17th century trading and pearl fishing town, which is Qatar's first-ever UNESCO Heritage site. Because of its power and wealth it attracted several invasions from Bahrain in the 18th century. Two areas have been reconstructed (the north house and the south house) and two further areas have been excavated – a souk area and a metal workers' shop. You can see the 11-hectare site clearly from the roof of Al Zubarah fort; just turn left at the fort and take any of the tracks leading from the right of the road.

## Al Zubarah Fort
### Zubarah, Madinat Al Shamal          qma.com.qa

Built in 1938, during the reign of Sheikh Abdullah bin Jassim Al Thani, this fort was erected beside the ruins of a much older fort. The impressive structure is square in shape, with high, thick walls, and has circular towers in three of its corners. The fort once served as a coastguard station and, until the mid 1980s, it was still being used by the military. It is a long drive from Doha, along rather bumpy roads, so it is probably better to visit this fort if you're already in the area.

Exploring

### Inland Sea (Khor Al Adaid)
South-east Qatar

Khor Al Adaid, better known as the 'Inland Sea', is an area of outstanding natural beauty. It's about 60km south of Doha and can only be reached in a 4WD. It's also vital that you drive in convoy with at least one experienced off-road driver. The Inland Sea is an important area for resident and migratory bird species, such as flamingos, cormorants, waders, gulls and terns. Plans to make the Inland Sea a protected conservation area are under discussion.

### Oryx Farm
Al Shahaniya, West of Doha

Located in the Al Shahaniya region in central Qatar, this protected farm houses a herd of Arabian oryx, which were once on the brink of extinction. The oryx is the national animal of Qatar and this farm one of your best bets to admire these graceful creatures in their natural habitat. To visit this farm independently you need a special permit from the Ministry of Municipal Affairs and Agriculture, so it may be easier to go with a tour company.

### Umm Salal Mohammed Fort
Umm Salal Mohammed                              qma.com.qa

This rundown fortification was constructed as a residence for Sheikh Jasim Bin Mohammed during the late 19th and early 20th centuries. It is notable for its thick high walls and impressive facade. The fort is not open to the public as it is still inhabited, but you get to admire the beautiful exterior.

*Arabian oryx relaxing in the shade*

Exploring

Outside of Doha

# Tours & Sightseeing

**Forget huge buses – tours through Qatar are an intimate affair and offer an efficient and educational way to see the country and capital.**

Most of the tour companies offer similar packages of trips in and around Doha. The absolute must-do is an excursion to the desert and the Inland Sea, camping overnight if you can. Several companies have permanent Arabic tents pitched there in the cooler months and offer some exhilarating dune bashing, after which they will cook a barbecue dinner and bring out the shisha.

Because the tour companies are fairly small local operations they can be very flexible in arranging whatever you want to do. Remember, the bigger your party the cheaper it will be. Below are some of the most common tours, followed by a list of the best tour operators in the country.

## Boat Tours

Day or evening dhow cruises that either sail around Doha Bay or venture further afield to one of the small islands are very relaxing and give you the chance to see Doha from a whole new perspective. A traditional meal is provided and there may be music and entertainment too. The trips usually last around three or four hours. Boats leave from the dhow harbour off the Corniche. There are various options depending on how long you want to go for and how many people are in your group.

### Regatta Sailing Academy

Al Gassar

4442 4577
regattasailingacademy.com

The academy has a range of equipment suitable for sailors of all ages, including lasers, catamarans and sports boats. You can seek the advice of several fully qualified British Royal Yacht Association instructors, and get some pointers in the safety of the lagoon before progressing to the waters of Doha Bay. A detailed price list for tuition and boat hire is available on the website. **Map** 3 D2

## City Tours

If you are in Doha on a short visit or you want a crash course in finding your way around, then book a city tour of Doha. You will spend the day in an air-conditioned bus, with commentary provided by an English-speaking tour guide. The tours tend to cover the majority of the attractions listed in this book, including an in-depth tour of Souk Waqif and other must-see sights.

### Places Of Worship

Throughout the country there are several small mosques that are used by local Muslims. Non-Muslims are not necessarily forbidden from entering the mosques (although some, such as the Grand Mosque on Al Rayyan Road, are totally off limits), but it is unusual and there are no organised tours. To respect the Islamic faith, it may be better to appreciate the beauty of Qatar's mosques from the outside. If you do happen to gain access to the inside of a mosque, remember to dress conservatively.

## Country Tours

Several companies offer trips out of Doha. The Inland Sea is the most popular destination for a day trip or a night's camping in an Arabic tent. Several companies, such as Gulf Adventures, do a trip north of Doha that takes in Al Khor with its Corniche and dhow harbour, as well as forts, mangroves (where you can kayak) and an old sheikh's palace. They also offer a tour to Shahaniya, which includes the Sheikh Faisal Museum and Camel Racing Track. It can organise a group tour to Zekreet too, but the terrain is quite rough and there is a limit to where you can set up camp.

## Safari Tours

A desert safari is a must-do in Qatar, and plenty of tour companies offer this. You will be picked up in a powerful 4WD to head into the dunes for some thrilling off-road driving and spectacular scenery. Seatbelts are compulsory and, as you defy gravity by skimming round the edge of enormous sand dunes, you will understand why.

## Main Tour Operators

### Arabian Adventures
Al Asmakh St

4436 1461
arabianadventureqatar.net

A good range of tours is offered by Arabian Adventures, taking explorers on safari adventures, city tours and fishing trips. Its 'heritage tour' takes in the oryx and camel farm, while a desert safari offers the chance to explore the sand dunes in 4WD vehicles led by experienced Qatari guides.  **Map** 1 H5

### Black Pearl

4435 7333

Nr Buchanan Furniture, Salwa Rd, Abu Hamour   blackpearl.com

Providing all of the most common tours, Black Pearl specialises in desert safaris and dhow cruises. The company offers several desert packages, including buggy drives and overnight trips. The five hour dhow cruise is also popular.  **Map** 1 E5

### Gulf Adventures Tourism

4422 1888

29 Aspire Zone St, Baaya   gulf-adventures.com

Gulf Adventures provides a range of tours including an Inland Sea safari, complete with a Bedouin campsite on the beach. They also offer a four-day trip that explores the old towns in the region. Keen divers can embark on the 'dive and drive' tour, which takes in some of Qatar's best diving spots.  **Map** 3 B5

### Qatar International Adventures

4455 3954

Al Matar Al Qadeem St, Old Airport   qia-qatar.com

This is one of the few companies that organises trips to camel racetracks. If you really want to catch a race, be sure to confirm times from the company before booking. The company also offers most of the popular tours, including city tours, desert safaris and shopping tours.  **Map** 1 E5

### Qatar International Tours

4455 1141

Al Hail Bldg, Al Matar St, Old Airport   qittour.com

This operator focuses on culturally themed tours. Choose to stay in the city and learn about its history up close, or cruise out to the desert to experience the Bedouin way of life. QIT also provides desert safaris and overnight packages.  **Map** 3 E5

# Sports & Spas

| | |
|---|---|
| **Active Qatar** | **116** |
| **Spectator Sports** | **130** |
| **Spas** | **138** |

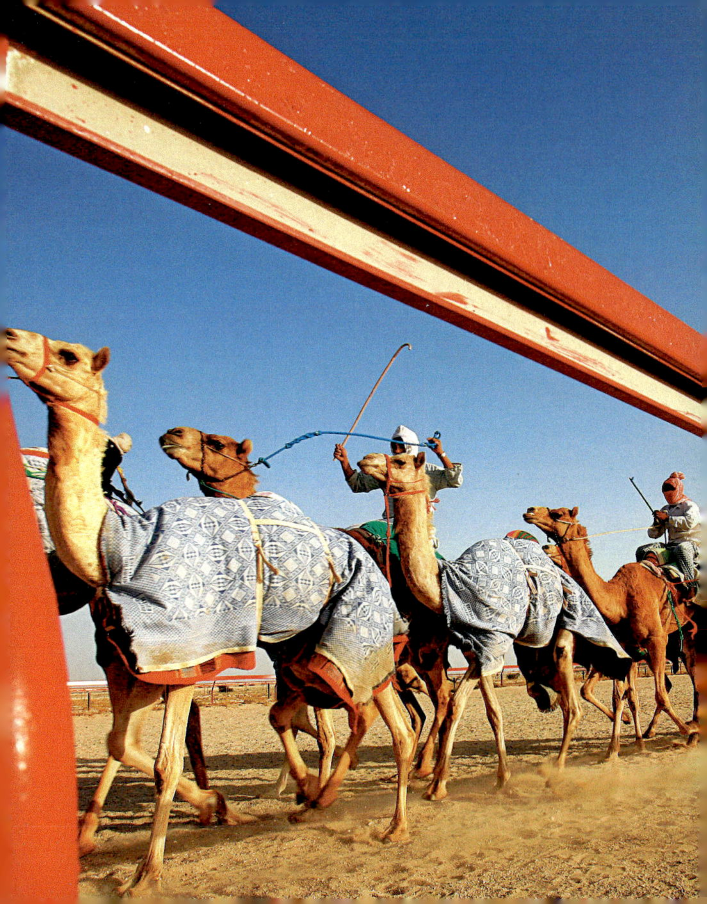

# Active Qatar

**Sports & Spas**

**Take advantage of the warm weather, fabulous beaches and varied landscape for dune bashing and watersports, or unwind at Qatar's luxurious spas.**

With the exception of a short period over the hot summer months when it becomes very humid, Qatar's location is ideal for participating in outdoor activities. You can also have a go at a variety of watersports; if you've always fancied trying a water-based activity, Qatar is the place to take it up. The great weather and warm sea should help tempt you into jumping on to a wakeboard, parasail or jet ski. There are also several good companies that offer diving and sailing trips for varying fees; costs will often include equipment hire and any training needed to participate.

If you prefer to be on dry land, a few tour operators offer desert safaris and dune-bashing tours, which can include overnight camping; this is a great way to get your adrenaline flowing whilst taking advantage of the region's diverse and spectacular landscape.

As Qatar won the bid to stage the 2022 FIFA World Cup, it has developed first-class facilities to generate sports-related tourism in the region, and has plans for eight new stadiums in time for the big event. Also, due to the country's focus on sports, football, tennis and motorsports, enthusiasts can take part in many sports and watch live action in state-of-the-art facilities. Aspire Zone is Qatar's renowned sporting destination,

Al Sadd Sports Club

Active Qatar | Sports & Spas

featuring an Olympic-sized pool, 34 outdoor gym stations, tennis courts, a 6km$^2$ running/walking track, horse trails, a bike track, football pitches and courts for both basketball and volleyball. On top of year-round events for the community, their Aspire Academy Centre of Excellence provides world-class development programmes for aspiring nationals.

If you're looking for ways to indulge, Qatar's luxurious spas and health clubs are largely based inside hotels and clubs, and provide a range of exclusive treatments and plenty of ways to pamper yourself in elegant surroundings.

## Camel Rides

### Sealine Beach Resort
Mesaieed

4476 5299
merweb.com

This is your chance to experience something that you probably wouldn't get to do in your home country; a camel ride along the beach. It costs QR 15 for a quick ride, and QR 100 for an hour (padded shorts are recommended for this option). You will, however, be restricted to the resort boundaries. **Map** 3 F6

## Camping

### Qatar International Tours
Al Hail Bldg, Matar St, Old Airport

4455 1141
qittour.com

Qatar International Tours provides all the camping equipment for tours including a fully furnished tent and water for the showers. A typical night starts with the lighting of a huge bonfire and then a chef prepares a sumptuous barbecue feast. A minimum of eight people are required. A band and belly dancer are available on request (for an extra charge). **Map** 3 E5

# Dhow Charters

You can find dhows to rent in Navigation Dhow Harbour (in front of the Day Palace on the Corniche). There are a large number of tourist dhows of various sizes for rent, some with catering facilities. Phone numbers are usually displayed on the boats. Look at the smaller, less expensive dhows where the road turns into a T-junction.

### Bay Club 4484 4852
InterContinental Doha, Al Gassar ichotelsgroup.com

You can charter a dhow for QR 335 per person, including lunch. The trip takes you to the nearby islands, or if you prefer you can just cruise along the Corniche. Trips can last anywhere between three and eight hours, depending on your preference (the price will vary accordingly). **Map** 3 D2

### Palm Tree Island Boat Company 4486 9151
Nr Sheraton Doha Resort &
 Convention Hotel, Al Dafna alaaelshazly@hotmail.com

Palm Tree was remodelled as a smaller island and many of the main facilities and features were removed, including the palm trees. Despite this, Palm Tree Island Boat Company conducts pleasant dhow trips around the island for a reasonable QR 20 for adults and QR 15 for children; this includes a soft drink and snack. No booking is required. **Map** 1 H2

# Diving

### Doha Sub Aqua Club (DSAC) 5589 0819
Nr Al Sharq Village & Spa, Al Khulaifat   dohasubaquaclub.com
DSAC offers a range of diving courses and awards British Sub Aqua Club qualifications. Shore dives are arranged to two artificial reefs that are still currently under construction. There are many wreck dives to be found. Trips to dive sites at Dukhan, Al Khor and the natural coral reefs in the Inland Sea are also organised. **Map** 1 K5

### Pearl Divers 4444 9553
Farig Al Nasser St, Al Sadd
Pearl Divers is a five-star PADI facility, where various diving qualifications certified by this international body are available. If you're new to diving, the instructors here can help you become a proficient diver in less than a week – after you've completed your training you will get the PADI Open Water Diver certification, which enables you to dive worldwide. Visit the Pearl Divers shop for a comprehensive range of diving equipment. **Map** 1 F6

### Q-Dive Marine Center 5531 9507
Souk Al Najada, Al Najada   qdive.net
This centre offers a full range of diving services and equipment rental. It arranges diving, snorkelling and fishing trips, either by a speedboat or on a classic dhow. It also offers a range of diving courses accredited under PADI.
**Map** 1 H5

# Fishing

The clear, warm waters of the Arabian Gulf provide rich fishing grounds. Kingfish and barracuda are just some of the potential catches of the day. The waterfront of the Corniche also provides an ideal spot. Alternatively, you can take part in an organised dhow trip through a tour company. If you wish to organise your own group, most of the dhows are berthed in Navigation Harbour on the Corniche (contacts on the vessel).

### Qatar International Tours
Al Hail Bldg, Matar St, Old Airport
4455 1141
qittour.com

A full-day fishing trip costs QR 180 on a traditional dhow, or QR 200 on a fishing boat. The price includes fishing line, bait, lunch and soft drinks. The highly experienced captain will bring you to the spots that yield the best catch. **Map** 3 E5

### Ronautica Middle East
Porto Arabia, The Pearl
4495 3894
ronauticame.com

This relatively new player on the fishing circuit offers an 8.5m luxurious fishing boat that can fit up to six people. Equipment is provided and you can choose the length of your session.
**Map** 3 D2

# Golf

### Doha Golf Club
Al Jamiaa St, Al Egla
4496 0777
dohagolfclub.com

Doha Golf Club is open daily to all. It has a 7,312 yard, 18-hole Championship course and a floodlit nine-hole Academy course. It is also home to several restaurants, lounges and conference rooms. The club hosts the Qatar Masters tournament. **Map** 3 C1

## Horse Riding

### Qatar Racing & Equestrian Club  4480 8122
Al Rayyan Farm, New Al Rayyan  qrec.gov.qa

Qatar Racing & Equestrian Club offers riding tuition for all ages, conducted by qualified instructors. You'll need to complete an application form and pay a monthly subscription fee (QR 300), which entitles you to three lessons per week. A medical certificate confirming your fitness to ride is required. **Map** 3 A5

### Sealine Beach Resort  4476 5299
Mesaieed  merweb.com

At this resort you can enjoy a horse ride along the beach. Camel rides are also available (although you'll be guided on a lead). If you can ride, you can hire a horse unaccompanied for one hour for QR 150. However, you will be restricted to the resort boundaries. **Map** 3 F6

## Kayaking

### Sealine Beach Resort  4476 5299
Mesaieed  merweb.com

This resort is a haven for water fanatics as it offers many watersports from its beautiful stretch of private beach,

Sports & Spas

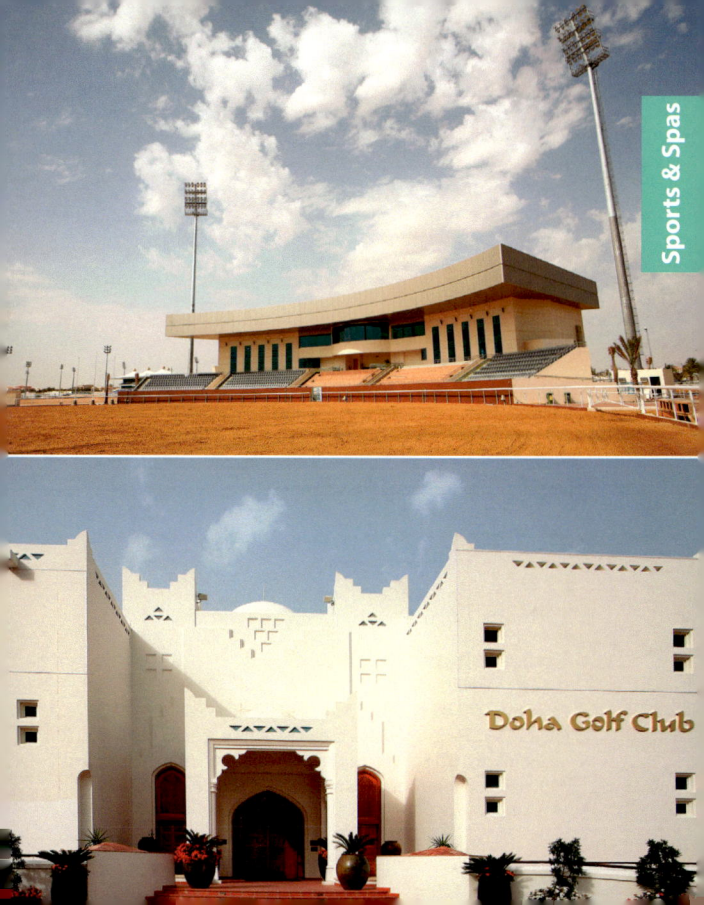

Doha Golf Club

including pedal boating, jet skiing and aqua cycles. You can hire a kayak for QR 50 per hour. Be sure to note that you are constrained to the resort shoreline area for safety reasons. Life jackets are provided.  **Map** 3 F6

## Kitesurfing

### Qatar Kitesurfing Club  5535 0336
Various locations

One of the fastest growing and most exciting sports on the water is kitesurfing, and Qatar is a great place to learn. The shallow waters of Zekrit Bay on the west coast and the similarly sheltered and shallow waters off West Bay in Doha are ideal locations for kitesurfing, especially if you are a beginner. If you've no experience it is essential to take lessons for safety reasons. Qatar Kitesurfing Club organises regular activities for those interested in learning from a registered instructor. They can also teach those who are more advanced and looking to perfect their skills.

## Parasailing

### Katara Cultural Village  4408 0000
Off Lusail St, Al Gassar  katara.net

From their private beach, a parasailing session here lasts for about 30 minutes, which is plenty of time to take in the beautiful coastline as you hover over the clear waters. Due to high demand, it is necessary to book in advance.  **Map** 3 D2

# Powerboating

### The Diplomatic Club
Al Gassar

4484 7444
thediplomaticclub.com

The Diplomatic Club has a 21-foot powerboat that can be hired for daytrips, fishing trips, waterskiing and island drop-offs. The hire includes an experienced captain. If you are waterskiing, instruction is available and safety cover is provided by trained lifeguards on jet skis. **Map** 3 D2

# Quad Bikes

### Sealine Beach Resort
Mesaieed

4476 5299
merweb.com

Tents are located all along the side of the road to Sealine Resort near Mesaieed, from which quad bikes of all sizes can be rented. Behind the tents are low dunes that you can practice on, but beware, especially if you have children with you; these are powerful machines, not toys, and they can be dangerous in inexperienced hands. Costs vary depending on the size of the machine, but expect to pay between QR 400 to QR 600 per hour. **Map** 3 F6

# Sailing

### Qatar Sailing & Rowing Federation
Ras Abu Abboud Rd, Al Khulaifat

4442 0305
qatarsailing.org

The Qatar Sailing & Rowing Federation is responsible for promoting sailing in the country, with the support of the

Doha Sailing Club. The club has a variety of boats suitable for all ages. Racing takes place at 1pm every Friday and regattas are organised regularly. Introductory lessons for beginners are given every Saturday (wind strength permitting) and reserving your spot will cost no more than a phone call to the club. **Map** 1 K5

### Regatta Sailing Academy 4442 4577
InterContinental Doha,
 Al Gassar regattasailingacademy.com

The academy has a range of equipment suitable for all ages, including lasers, catamarans and sports boats. You can seek the advice of fully qualified British Royal Yacht Association instructors and get some pointers in the safety of the lagoon before progressing to the waters of Doha Bay. **Map** 3 D2

## Sand Boarding
For thrills and spills, desert style, try sand boarding on the dunes. You won't reach the breakneck speeds of snow boarding and, if you do fall off, you land in lovely soft sand. This must-try activity is offered by most of the tour operators.

### Qatar International Tours 4455 1141
Al Hail Bldg, Matar St, Old Airport qittour.com

Whether you choose to go on the half-day or full-day desert safari with Qatar International Tours, you'll have the opportunity to try your hand at sand skiing. A half-day tour lasts four hours and costs QR 250 per person and includes a number of activities. A full-day tour costs QR

300 and lasts eight hours. A group of four participants are required for each tour. **Map** 3 E5

# Snorkelling

### Q-Dive Marine Center
Souk Al Najada, Al Najada

5531 9507
qdive.net

Apart from being a top-class dive centre, Q-Dive also offers snorkelling trips. Its fully-trained staff are on hand for those who are new to snorkelling and Q-Dive will also arrange equipment hire. There are weekly trips to either the southern or northern waters off Qatar's coast. Day trips are available to Safliya Island. **Map** 1 H5

# Wadi & Dune Bashing

Qatar boasts some impressive sand dunes, reaching heights of nearly 50 metres. With a skilled driver behind the wheel, you can spend a thrilling afternoon racing up sand dunes and navigating your way down the other side. Unless you are extremely experienced, it is safer to enlist the help of one of the tour operators than to attempt dune bashing yourself. If you do go off into the desert in your own vehicle, always adhere to safety precautions and, most importantly, travel in convoy.

### Gulf Adventures Tourism
29 Aspire Zone St, Baaya

4422 1888
gulf-adventures.com

Gulf Adventures' comprehensive range of tours includes desert safaris and camping trips. For the ultimate desert safari, take the overnight desert tour, which includes a stay in a Bedouin campsite after you've spent the day dune bashing. A dune discovery day tour is also offered daily for QR 240 per person. **Map** 1 A6

### Qatar International Tours
Al Hail Bldg, Matar St, Old Airport

4455 1141
qittour.com

Experience the thrill of riding up and over dunes and through rugged wadis on an organised trip with Qatar International Tours. You can choose from a half-day tour (four hours at QR 250 per person) or a full-day tour (which lasts eight hours and costs QR 300 each). There must be a minimum of four participants per trip. **Map** 3 E5

## Wakeboarding

### Ronautica Middle East
Porto Arabia, The Pearl

4495 3894
ronauticame.com

There's a wide range of watersports, including wakeboarding, waterskiing, wake skating and knee boarding, available for adults and children through Ronautica Middle East. The pick-up point is located inside the marina at Porto Arabia. Wakeboarding around The Pearl, in particular, makes for a unique and thrilling experience. There is space for six guests on board this watersport specific speedboat and the skipper is more than happy to teach the basics to beginners, and provide guidance for the more experienced. All equipment, wetsuits and refreshments will be provided. There is also a catering package available upon request. **Map** 3 D2

### The Diplomatic Club

4484 7444
thediplomaticclub.com

Al Gassar

A range of watersports is available here, and non-members can use the facilities too. Wakeboarding is available for adults and children. It costs QR 250 per hour and there is an extra charge for instruction of QR 125. All watersports are available from 9am to just before sunset. **Map** 3 D2

Sports & Spas

# Spectator Sports

**Qatar features some of the finest sports stadiums in the world, part of a strategy to develop the nation into a regional hub for sports-related tourism.**

Aspire Zone is Qatar's unique sports destination and reflects the country's commitment to community sport and sports-related tourism. With over 2.5 km$^2$ of elite facilities and 34 outdoor gym stations, there is an active annual calendar of fitness events, tournaments and programmes for both the community and aspiring athletes. The impressive Aspire Park boasts a running track, horse and bike circuits, several football pitches, as well as basketball and volleyball courts.

Meanwhile, the Aspire Academy Centre of Excellence was established in 2004 to develop Qatar's most talented pool of nationals. Supported by top-class coaches and programmes, athletes also gain experience through international events organised by Aspire; the venue features first-rate competition areas and spectator facilities. Depending on schedules, you may be able to see some of the world's top high divers or gymnasts in action alongside other sports.

As in many countries, the dominant sport is football, with motorsports coming a close second in popularity. The premium facilities for watching football are very good; even comparable with some of the sport's top stadia. Other sports have not been neglected either: billions of riyals have been spent on spectator facilities, particularly in the case of tennis, badminton and motorsports.

Aspire Zone offers world-class sporting and active lifestyle facilities

Spectator Sports | Sports & Spas

Regular sporting fixtures are not guaranteed to take place at a specific time but can usually be pinned down to within a month. Timing is often further complicated by the fact that the holy month of Ramadan usually arrives 12 days earlier each year.

## Camel Racing

Camel racing is big in Qatar. The centre of the sport is Shahaniyah, which is about 20 kilometres west of Doha, on the road to Dukhan. Here lies a collection of camel breeding farms and studs, complete with a 10 kilometre camel-racing track and grandstand (Qatar Camel Racing Committee, Shahaniyah Race Track, 4487 2028).

You can watch a race from the stands or, for a more thrilling experience, join the owners who use the outer track to follow their animals around in an attempt to encourage them to win. The latter option is an exciting experience, but don't get too close, as riding standards are a little worrying.

## Cycling

The international highlight of this sport is the gruelling Tour de France, but the best competitors also regularly participate in the Tour of Qatar. While flatter and smaller than France, Qatar is certainly much hotter, even in the cooler months of January or February when the event is usually scheduled. Roads are closed while the race is taking place and all you have to do is turn up. The competition always ends at the Corniche. Visit the Tour de France website (letour.fr) for more information on the Qatar event, including course maps.

# Equestrian Sports

Horse racing in Qatar takes place throughout the winter months at the impressive Qatar Racing & Equestrian Club. The club also caters for other forms of equestrian sport including an Arabian horse show in March, (the local press will provide the exact timings of the event). The Desert Marathon takes place during the relatively cooler winter months, south of Mesaieed. A course is laid in the valleys between the sand dunes and riders from around the world compete in the event. To watch this sport all you need is a 4WD vehicle and a picnic. Just sit in the desert and wait for the riders to pass by. Keep an eye on the local press for timings.

### Qatar Racing & Equestrian Club   4480 8122
Al Rayyan Farm, New Al Rayyan   qrec.gov.qa

Races are scheduled every Thursday from about 4pm until about 9pm, entry is completely free of charge. Although gambling is prohibited, race-goers can put their names into free raffles based on what they think the winning horse will be. Prizes are substantial and often include cars. The course is also floodlit, with good coverage on huge TV screens.
**Map** 3 A5

# Football

There is no spectator sport in Qatar bigger than football. Domestic competition consists of 18 teams, which are formed into two leagues (visit the Qatar Football Association's website, qfa.com.qa/en, for information.) The season runs throughout the cooler months from October to April.

## Spectator Sports

International matches and friendly tours are usually played at the stadiums belonging to the larger Q-League teams, such as Al Arabi, Al Sadd, and Rayyan. Football fans from overseas can watch a game for a meagre amount, ranging from free to QR 10 if it happens to be an international match.

Football violence is unheard of – but when a major match is won, fans tend to leap into their 4WDs and drive up and down Doha Corniche with revellers standing on car roofs, revving their engines and burning up their tyres; it is not malicious, but it's best avoided.

> ### World Cup 2022
> In December 2010, FIFA amazed the world by awarding the bid to host the 2022 football World Cup to Qatar. The tiny Gulf state is the first Arab country to receive the bid, and it is taking its role as host seriously, pouring billions into building the infrastructure needed to sustain the World Cup. The debate about the extreme heat, and when best to schedule kick off, is ongoing.

## Golf

In January each year the Doha Golf Club (4493 0777, dohagolfclub.com) in West Bay hosts the Commercial Bank Qatar Masters on its pleasant course, designed by Peter Harradine. The event, like many in the region, offers major prize money and attracts some of the world's best players. It is not unknown for local golf aficionados to spend part of their annual leave watching the Masters – it's an opportunity to watch world class golf at close quarters without the usual hindrance of crowds. The governing body is the Qatar Golf Association (4483 7815, qga.com.qa).

## Motorsports

Designed primarily as a motorcycle track, Losail hosts a round of the Superbike World Championship (worldsbk.com), which is normally held in February. It is also the setting for the Qatar heat of the MotoGP (motogp.com), usually staged in March. Follow the new Al Khor road from Doha for about 10 kilometres and the purpose-built Losail racetrack, is signposted on your right. Spectators are restricted to the large stand on the fast starting and finishing straight, and visibility can be obscured by the pit buildings opposite. However, the stand does provide ample shade from the sun and a good view of the action in the pits.

The track is occasionally used for car racing, and rounds of the Grand Prix Masters series (themastersseries.com) have been held here. Entrance fees are low, but this depends on the status of the event taking place.

### Qatar International Rally
Various locations

4437 9884
qmmf.com

The highlight of motor rallying is the Qatar International Rally. This event takes place over three days in January. The location of the rally sites, which take full advantage of the country's desert terrain, varies from year to year and you will need to keep an eye on the local press for information about its location.

**Qatar Motor & Motorcycle Federation**  4437 9884
Bldg 59, Salwa Rd, Rawdat Al Khail  circuitlosail.com

Qatar Motor & Motorcycle Federation is the governing body for motorsports in Qatar, and holds several car and motorcycle rallies throughout the year. The federation is always on the lookout for keen volunteers who can help with the events. Visit the website to download a volunteer application form.  **Map** 1 F5

## Powerboat Racing

This is a popular sport in Qatar, run under the umbrella of the Qatar Marine Sports Federation (QMSF), which organises world-class events in powerboat racing and equips local sportsmen to take part in international competitions. There are no membership fees but registration fees are required to take part in the events. The leading powerboat sports here are Class 1 Offshore Powerboat Racing and Formula 2000 Powerboat Racing (Boat GP). Every year the QMSF organises two rounds of Class 1 Offshore Powerboat Racing, one round of Formula 2000 Powerboat Racing and one round of the Middle East Formula 2000 Powerboat Championships. For more information visit the QMSF website, qmsf.org, or call 4404 8667.

## Squash

The Qatar Classic Squash Championship (qatarsquash.com) usually attracts the cream of the world's players to the Khalifa Tennis Stadium (4440 9666), but the timing of the event seems to vary (check the website for updates.)

## Tennis

You can see the biggest tennis stars here for a negligible price and, unless it is a final match, you will have the pick of the seats. Men compete in the annual Qatar ExxonMobil Open (qatartennis.org) which takes place in late December or early January. Prize money is substantial and consequently all the best players turn up. The women's equivalent, the Qatar Total Open (qatartennis.org), commences a month after the men's competition. Matches for both take place in Khalifa Tennis Stadium (4440 9666). For more information on the tournaments see the website of the Qatar Tennis Federation (qatartennis.org) or call 4483 2991.

**Sports & Spas**

## Spas

**Sports & Spas**

Relax and recharge at one of Doha's luxury hotel spas, which offer a multitude of pampering treatments and ways for you to unwind.

### Angsana Spa
4434 3152
Wyndham Grand Regency Al Sadd   angsanaspa.com

Situated in the Grand Regency Hotel, the Angsana Spa is a calming escape from the hustle and bustle of modern city life. Choose from a lengthy list of Asian-influenced treatments that include everything from perfect anti-ageing facials to therapeutic body massages and invigorating body polishes derived from green tea and other natural sources.
**Map** 1 E4

### Bliss Spa
4453 5555
W Doha Hotel & Residences
Al Dafna   blissworld.com

From the cheerful welcome at the door to the luxuriously soft robes, Bliss is an oasis of calm and offers a unique concept in Qatar. With its peaceful and calming interior and its stylish, white leather opulence, it's like stepping into a parallel universe. Housed in the so-hip-it-hurts W Hotel, it has a luxury nail lounge with manicure and pedicure stations equipped with personal TVs and cosy sofas. Stand out treatments include the Blissage 75 massage and the Triple Oxygen Treatment Facial. Bliss might not be cheap, but for an escape from Doha's dusty streets, it's worth it.   **Map** 1 H1

### Jaula Spa

Grand Hyatt Doha Al Gassar

4448 1056
doha.grand.hyatt.com

Luxurious and resplendent, Jaula offers a truly outstanding spa experience. Guests utilise private, purpose-built suites in which everything from changing and showering to therapy is performed, letting you escape into your own haven of welcome solitude. Exceptional treatments promote wellness and harmony and are delivered by skilled staff who use all-natural products from marine and botanical sources that focus on rejuvenation, hydration and deep relaxation. Massages, facials, scrubs, wraps and waxing are all on offer, using enriching oils, minerals, clays, salts, seaweeds and algae. **Map** 3 D1

### Remede Spa, St Regis Doha

St Regis Doha, Al Gassar

4446 0300
stregisdoha.com

This spa covers 1,400 square metres and offers 22 treatment rooms, pre- and post-treatment lounges, as well as male and female relaxation pools and steam rooms, making it one of the largest spas in Doha. Try the cooling pearl facial with white lotus stem cells and oxygen. **Map** 3 D2

### The Spa, Ritz-Carlton Doha

Ritz-Carlton Doha Al Gassar

4484 8173
ritzcarlton.com

Offering complete luxury for men and women, this spa features seven private treatment rooms, as well as a sauna, a steam room, an indoor pool and roman baths. All treatments are excellent, but the Oriental massage and hydrotherapy deserve a special mention. There are separate facilities for

men and women. The spa also offers a range of day and overnight packages; see the website for more details.
**Map** 3 D1

### Six Senses Spa  4425 6999
Sharq Village & Spa
Al Khulaifat  sixsenses.com/six-senses-spas

This impressive spa has 23 treatment rooms to choose from, together with an impressive menu. The spa is traditionally decorated, in luxurious surroundings, with plunge pools, saunas and relaxation rooms. A wide range of facial and body treatments are available here, including Balinese, Swedish and aromatherapy. The spa offers a number of packages to suit all needs, with the inclusion of relaxing classes such as tai chi and meditation. Check their website for a spa menu and further information. **Map** 1 K5

### Spa & Wellness Centre  4494 8801
Four Seasons Hotel
Al Dafna  fourseasons.com/doha

The unique facilities in this state-of-the-art spa include a hydrotherapy lounge and pool, cool and warm plunge pools, a reflexology foot bath, heated laconium beds, a colour therapy room and a meditation room. Other treatments offered include wraps, scrubs and Thai massage. There are separate areas for men and women and you can also hire your own private spa suite complete with a whirlpool. Complimentary refreshments are offered in the relaxation areas. **Map** 1 H1

Sports & Spas

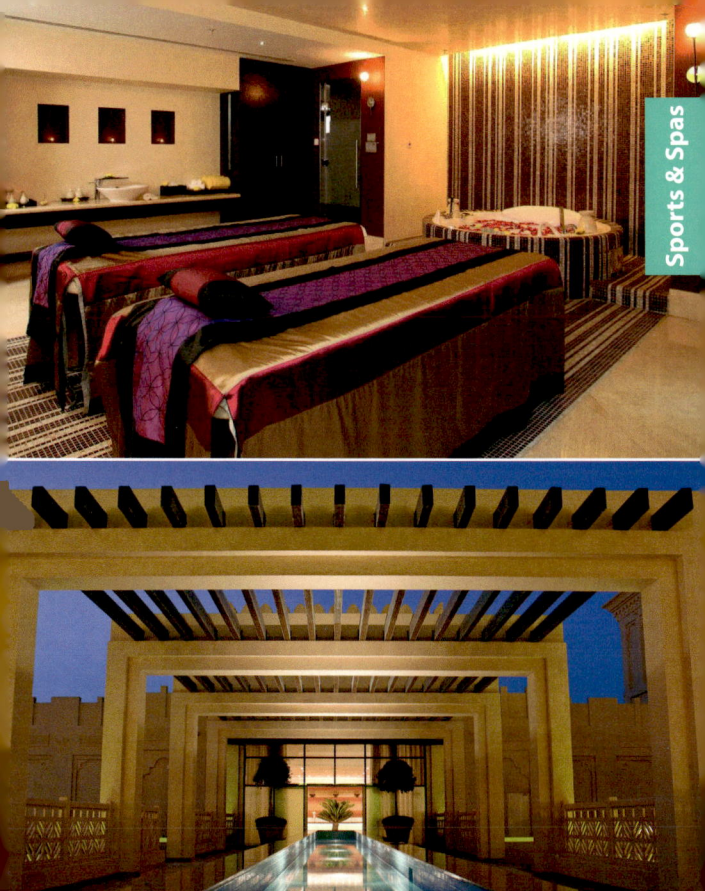

# Shopping

| | |
|---|---|
| **Shopping In Qatar** | **144** |
| **Hotspots** | **146** |
| **Markets & Souks** | **148** |
| **Shopping Malls** | **154** |
| **Department Stores** | **160** |
| **Where To Go For...** | **162** |

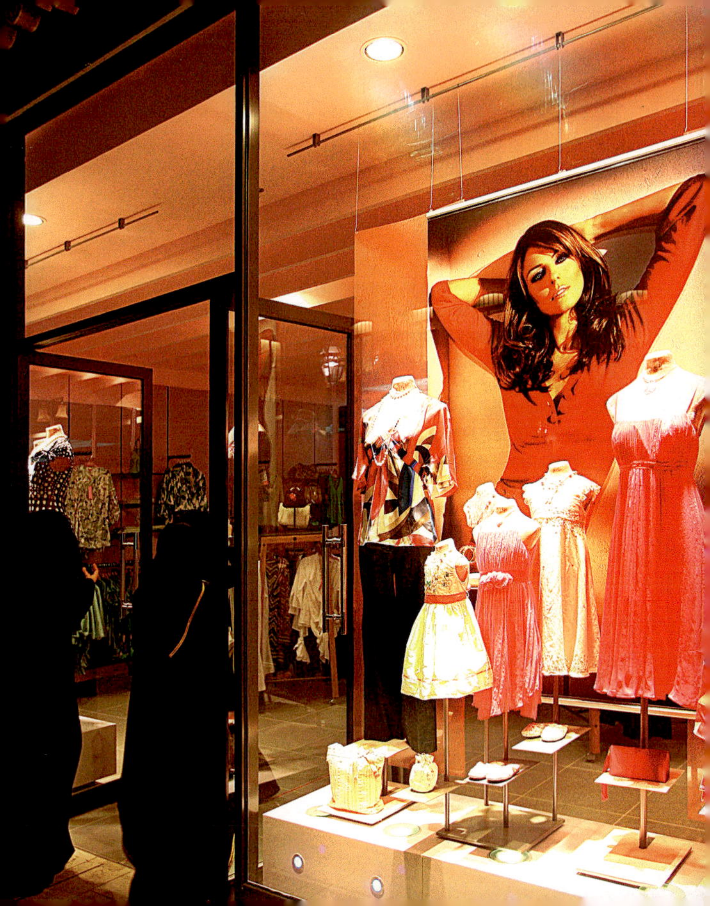

# Shopping In Qatar

**Whether you decide to splurge in luxurious malls or wander around authentic souks, Qatar has something for everyone.**

The shopping scene in Qatar has developed a great deal over the years – as the population has expanded, so has the retail potential. Many international brands and retailers have taken the opportunity to move into a new and growing market. From high-end brand name boutiques right down to funky little one-person stores in the souks, traditional and modern blend together to bring surprises and bargains. Qatar should keep most shopaholics happily swiping their credit cards. Big shopping centres all house major international brands, and because there is no sales tax or VAT you might find some things cheaper than in your home country, although this is not always the case.

Qatar's many large malls can service just about every shopping need you have, and then some. The latest shopping mall to open its doors is the Lagoona Mall located within ZigZag Towers. It's the new address for high-end fashion and fine dining establishments with the giant Fifty One East department store flanking one end of the mall. Elsewhere, City Center Doha and Landmark Shopping Mall are among your other options for retail therapy. Many of the bigger malls feature department stores that sell a good range of cosmetics, clothing and jewellery. The Pearl has also become a prime location for high-end designer retailers and boutique shops with Hermes, Armani, Vera Wang, MaxMara, Jimmy Choo and Alexander McQueen all around the marina area of Porto Arabia.

Malls are not concentrated in one area of Doha; you'll find them scattered around the city and because of traffic, it's best to reserve enough time for the 'getting there' part if you're planning a multi-mall shopping trip. That said, with plentiful parking and reasonably priced taxis, mall hopping can be relatively drama free.

A visit to the traditional markets is a must. Many are clustered together near the Souk Waqif area so you can wander from one to the other quite easily. Souk Waqif is a landmark in Doha and arguably one of the most beautiful souks in the Middle East. There is a huge range of shops and the choices are growing. It's not just a shopping destination – dozens of great eateries have opened their doors in the area as well, and there are traditional dance performances and entertainment during the cooler months.

### Shops Outside Doha

Shopping outside of Doha is less appealing than in the capital; luxury malls and interesting souks are few and far between, although new and growing communities in Al Khor and Al Wakra signal a future change. If you can't find what you're looking for in Doha, chances are you won't find it in the surrounding area either, so a trip to nearby Dubai or Abu Dhabi might be the answer.

# Hotspots

**For a shopping experience beyond the malls, try exploring the eclectic mix of stores and markets near Salwa Road.**

In general, malls are the most popular areas to shop; not just because of the variety of well-known stores, but also because in summer they are cool thanks to powerful air-conditioning.

There are, however, a handful of other places to indulge in retail therapy. Salwa Road (Map 1 F5) is home to various independent outlets that are frequented by all kinds of shoppers. You'll find Jarir Bookstore (4444 0212), Apollo Furniture (4468 9522) and Skate Shack (4469 2532), to name just a few. Salwa Road is famous for its many furniture shops, although most of the stock is for those with rather flamboyant tastes. One of the nice things about shopping on Salwa Road is the availability of parking spaces.

Al Mirqab Street (Map1 E6) is another popular shopping destination. It has several fabric shops and tailors, a great art shop, stores where you can get upholstery or have curtains made, phone shops, toy shops and a few pharmacies.

Al Sadd Street (Map 1 D5) also has a number of interesting shops, as well as the newly opened Royal Plaza shopping centre.

The souk areas are popular and offer a vibrant glimpse into traditional life. The food and fabric souks are popular with all nationalities. The Musheirib (Map1 G5) area (better known as the Sofitel shopping complex) has numerous shops selling everything from cheap fabric to top-of-the-range TVs. It is very busy at weekends though, and parking is a nightmare.

The Central Market (Map 3 B6) area along Salwa Road is where you will find the food and livestock markets. This area is well worth a visit every now and then to stock up on fruit, vegetables and fresh fish.

While many people choose to go to the shopping malls, especially during the summer months, visiting the souks is still a great experience. With its bustling activity and quirky charm, it's worthwhile visiting at least once.

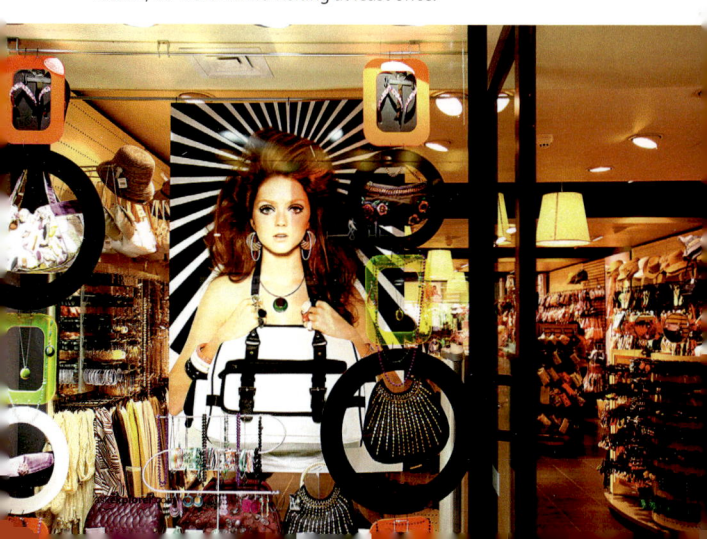

**Shopping**

**Shopping**

# Markets & Souks

**Pick up anything from stuffed camels to traditional spices in Doha's souks; these bustling markets offer a chance to experience a fragment of local life.**

The souks in Doha sell a huge range of items. Much of what you can buy in the souks can also be found in shopping centres and supermarkets but, as a general rule, souks tend to be cheaper because you have the power of bargaining.

On the whole, these bustling markets are fascinating, not only from a shopper's point of view (you could spend an entire morning rummaging around), but also because of the cultural experience – it's a good chance to get up close and personal with a traditional form of business.

Bargaining is a skill that should be practised and enjoyed. Vendors are friendly and eager to make a sale, and they expect a bit of negotiating from their customers. Shop around first so that you know what something is worth, and use that as a starting point for your negotiations.

Remember that souks are traditional areas often predominately populated by men, so it's wise for women to dress conservatively, with shoulders and legs covered. If you wear something tight or revealing then be prepared to be gawked at.

Souk Waqif (the Old Souk) is an extraordinary place, where you can buy a traditional Qatari outfit in one store and then walk up the street to eat at a Moroccan restaurant before picking up some kitchen appliances on your way home. Outside of Souk Waqif, all of Doha's main souks (the Omani Market, Fruit and Vegetable Market, Fish Market and Animal Market) are situated in the same area south-west of the city on Salwa Road.

### Omani Market
#### Nr Wholesale Market, Abu Hamour
The Omani Market sells plants, pots, garden materials and a selection of woven mats and baskets, which are imported from Oman and, increasingly, Iran and India. There are also a few stalls selling nuts and dates. There isn't a huge choice of pots, but it is worth taking the time to browse through all the plants. Don't forget to bargain with the friendly and enthusiastic vendors for a better price. There are a number of plant nurseries in the surrounding area selling pots and plants.  **Map** 3 B6

### Thursday & Friday Market
#### Salwa Rd, Ain Khaled
Located opposite the Fish Market, this market is only operational on two days of the week, in the evenings. In its heyday, it was one of the busiest markets in the city. But sadly, after a fire two years ago, it is now a shadow of its former self. Vendors sell assorted goods such as perfume, clothes, carpets, fabric and household items. There are a few permanent shops in the area selling similar items, but the selection is poor compared with what you will find in the market.  **Map** 3 B6

### Souk Waqif

**Off Grand Hamad St, Al Jasra**

With its cobblestone labyrinth of alleyways, mud walls and wooden beams, it's hard to believe this impressive version of Souk Waqif is just a few years old. The souk's history dates back to when Doha was a tiny village divided by Wadi Mishireb. The actual site of Souk Waqif (or to taxi drivers the 'old souk') sits between Al Souk Street and Grand Hamad Street. The area used to be run down until the government restored it to its original glory in 2004.

The souk's open-air area hosts cultural activities, entertainment and dining. Locals and residents alike head here for items ranging from cooking pots to traditional dress. The souk is known for its spice market, offering pungent delicacies from around the Gulf, Middle East and Asia. Other offerings include honey from Yemen, pashminas from Kashmir and 'antiques' from India. Along the central outdoor area you can find men weaving traditional Bedouin blankets and cushion covers for majlis style furniture. The area also includes the Waqif Art Centre. Most stalls open in the morning but it's livelier after 4pm. **Map** 1 H4

# Around Souk Waqif

### Gold Souk

With gold reaching record prices around the globe, it remains a bargain commodity in this part of the world. Many expats prefer to take gold rather than cash back to their home country. The government regulates the purity of gold, so you

*Antiques shop at Souk Waqif*

Shopping

Markets & Souks

askexplorer.com  151

can be assured it's all great quality. The gold on display here ranges from the spectacular Indian and Arab bridal jewellery through to humble bracelets, all in 18 carat or 22 carat. The Gold Souk can be found just off Ali Bin Abdullah Street.

### Souk Al Ahmed, Souk Al Dira & Souk Al Asiery

These three souks are great stops for those who wish to recreate the latest catwalk look or design their own creations. Souk Al Ahmed, also known as the 'bridal souk', is an air-conditioned two storey building off Grand Hamed Street that houses dozens of specialist bridal tailors. Souk Al Dira, which is also known as the 'button and bow souk', is the place to buy fabric by the metre. You'll find a good range of material here from simple cotton right through to the finest silk. Stores in this souk also sell all manner of accoutrements to ensure you have everything you need to make a one-of-a-kind creation. Much of the current structure was destroyed by fire in October 2009 but, fortunately, a good section of the souk survived. Souk Al Asiery is a cheaper version of souks Al Ahmed and Al Dira, which are all located on Al Ahmed Street. Souk Al Asiery is the place to go to find all kinds of fabrics at knockdown prices.

### Souk Al Jabor

You will find everything from perfume, toys, and cheap shoes to tacky souvenirs in this jumble of a souk. Located on Al Ahmed Street, you will need to take your patience with you and be prepared to spend some time rummaging around to find the things you need.

Souk Waqif

### Souk Haraj

This quiet little gem on Al Mansoura Street is as close as Doha gets to a flea market. Shops here sell locally made furniture at great prices. The carpentry and metalwork stores located just off the main square also sell curtains, carpets and assorted items of furniture. The majority of the furniture is imported from India and Pakistan and business is conducted off the back of trucks and trailers. You can also pick up second-hand crockery, jewellery and tools.

### Souk Nasser Bin Saif

This is the electronics souk, where you can find everything a new home requires. CDs, DVDs and even the odd audio tape are on sale here.

# Shopping Malls

When the heat is on, Qataris head indoors – and the luxurious air-conditioned malls filled with high fashion are a perfect refuge.

### Al Asmakh Mall                                  4444 2401
**Al Sadd**

Al Asmakh Mall, also called Centrepoint, is the little mall with big shops. Babyshop has children's toys for all ages, playhouses, cots, beds and clothing. Close by you'll find Splash, with very reasonably priced clothes, and Shoe Mart with a broad selection for children and adults. The Home Centre has a good range of furniture and takes up a large portion of the top floor. Opposite Home Centre is a small children's play area called Fun City, which is a great distraction for bored kids and tired parents. **Map** 1 E5

### City Center Doha                               4483 9990
**Al Dafna**

You could spend an entire day in City Center and still not get to experience everything it has to offer. The centre features outlets selling a variety of international and local merchandise. Numerous cafes are scattered throughout the mall. There are plenty of ways to entertain kids including an ice rink and a ten-pin bowling alley. There is also a spa and a ladies' salon, a gym and a 14-screen cinema. City Center is open from 10am to 10pm Saturday to Thursday, and from 2pm to10pm on Fridays. **Map** 1 G1

خيارات أكثر
من أي وقت!
More choice
than ever!
سيتي سنتر
CITY
CENTER
Branch of Aamal Company

## Shopping Malls

### Hyatt Plaza
Baaya  
4499 9666  
hyattplaza.com

You'll recognise Hyatt Plaza from the enormous shopping trolley outside, which you can see from the roundabout by Khalifa Stadium. The trolley is an advert for Geant (4469 2996), the excellent supermarket located in the centre. This mall is smaller in comparison to some of the newer ones, but there is a smattering of high-street brands, including The Body Shop and Mothercare, while Paris Gallery stocks the designer labels. **Map** 3 A5

### Lagoona Mall
Al Gassar  
4433 5555  
lagoonamall.com

Doha's latest mall is an exciting addition to the West Bay shopping scene. Located at the base of the iconic Zig Zag Towers, the gigantic mall spans 128,000 square meters and houses some 160+ shops and an atmospheric European-style piazza, which is surrounded by some great cafes and restaurants. The mall is anchored by two high-end department stores that specialise in luxury brands: Fifty One East and Paris Gallery, but you'll also find a good selection of high street chains such as Mango and Springfield that stock everyday fashions at reasonable prices. **Map** 3 D1

### Landmark Mall
Umm Lekhba  
4487 5222  
landmarkdoha.com

This mall is in the style of a Qatari castle. Inside you'll find a variety of international and local stores, renowned brands and the latest worldwide fashion. The mall is also popular for its two large UK department stores Marks & Spencer and Bhs. The mall also has a foodcourt with typical fastfood outlets like McDonald's and Subway, but there are a few restaurants including TGI Friday's and Pizza Express. Landmark hosts a number of art exhibitions and events, and during special occasions and festivals (like Eid) there is plenty of family entertainment within the mall. Most of the shops open at either 9am or 10am and close at 11pm. On Fridays, all shops open at 1.30pm.  **Map** 3 B3

### The Mall
Old Airport

4467 8888
themalldoha.com

The Mall was the first shopping centre to open in Doha, in the mid 1990s. Since then it has grown into one of the most popular places for shopping. Radio Shack, Paul Frank, Birkenstock, Mont Blanc, Givenchy and Monsoon are among the outlets here. There is a three-screen cinema showing the latest American, European and Arabic films.  **Map** 3 D5

### The Pearl Qatar
North of West Bay

4495 3888
thepearlqatar.com

While this is less like a traditional shopping mall, The Pearl is worth a visit just to surround yourself with luxury. There is an extraordinary collection of high-end designer retailers. If your Louboutins need a rest, you can stop for a break at the world famous Alison Nelson's Chocolate Bar, or sip an espresso on the boardwalk while watching the extravagant yachts sail by. Evening visitors can also choose from a range of world-class, fine dining options.  **Map** 3 D2

## Shopping Malls

### Royal Plaza
Al Sadd

4413 0000
royalplazadoha.com

This luxury mall offers a white glove service where you can pre-book a gentleman to assist with your shopping and carry all those bags. Small but perfectly formed, its three retail levels consist of boutiques such as Cartier, Mont Blanc, Levi's, Givenchy and Morgan, to name a few. There are a variety of features available including a gift idea service, limousine services, baby changing facilities, complimentary strollers, lost and found, shoe polishing, mobile recharging and wheelchairs. The art deco-style Cinema Palace and is a plush place to catch the latest English, Arabic and Hindi releases.
**Map** 1 E5

### Villaggio Mall
Baaya

4413 5222
villaggioqatar.com

One of the most unique malls in Doha, Villaggio Mall is located in the shadow of Aspire's Torch Hotel, next to the Khalifa Stadium. As you pass through the doors you are transported to an Italian village on the sea with gondola rides on the canal and the illusion of blue skies between villas and storefronts. Villaggio comes complete with cafes, among which are Cafe Vergnano, Columbus Cafe and Paul, as well as all the standard fastfood chains and a handful of restaurants ranging from Pizza Express to Indian eatery Asha's. As for the shopping, you can buy just about anything here. There's a huge Carrefour for everyday essentials, Virgin Megastore for entertainment, the largest Quiksilver in the region and every conceivable brand name store in between.  **Map** 3 A5

Shopping

Shopping Malls

# Department Stores

Department stores here may pale in comparison to the colossal shopping centres in Europe or America, but they are still good for one-stop shopping.

### Blue Salon
4446 6111
Suhaim Bin Hamad St, Fereej Bin Mahmoud  bluesalon.com
Blue Salon carries a range of brands including Armani, Aigner and Diesel. The shop sells the typical products found in a department store, including linen, electronic goods and men's and women's fashion.  **Map** 1 F5

### Fifty One East
4425 7777
City Center Doha, Al Dafna  51east.com.qa
Fifty One East is Qatar's premier luxury department store catering to the needs of Doha's elite. With a number of other branches, one in Al Maha Centre, another on Salwa Road and the latest one inside Lagoona Mall, it is a leading fashion, jewellery and electronics retailer in Qatar. The store offers one of the widest selections of the most prestigious brands and products.  **Map** 1 H1

### Highland
4467 8678
The Mall, Old Airport
Highland sells a variety of items including high-end cosmetics and perfumes, clothing and luggage. The children's section caters to younger kids. This eclectic store also has an

interesting souvenir section where you can buy a crystal falcon if your heart so desires it.  **Map** 3 E5

### Marks & Spencer  4488 0101
Landmark Shopping Mall, Umm Lekhba  marksandspencerme.com

British stalwart Marks & Spencer is a great department store that is very popular with both expats and locals. There is a wide selection of fashion items for the whole family. The children's clothes range from newborns right up to trendy teens. The ladies' section has a lovely range of the latest fashion and clothes are available from petite to plus-size.
**Map** 3 B3

### Merch  4467 4314
The Mall, Old Aiport

Merch is another high-end department store, and its defining feature is its enviable cosmetic and perfume section, which holds a variety of international brands. There is another branch of the store on Salwa Road (4465 8656).
**Map** 3 E5

### Salam  4448 5555
Maysaloun St, Al Dafna  salaminternational.com

Salam is a well-known name in this part of the world: its department stores, Salam Plaza and Salam Studio (The Mall), carry a wide range of good quality merchandise including clothing, cosmetics, luggage and household goods.  **Map** 1 G1

## Where To Go For...

*Shopping*

### Carpets

Most carpets sold in Qatar have been made in countries such as Iran, India, Pakistan or China. Persian carpets are regarded as being the best investment. The price of an original Persian carpet can reach tens of thousands of riyals. They are usually extremely attractive and they take years to make. Hand-made carpets are more valuable than machine-made ones and silk is more expensive than wool. The more knots per square metre, the better the carpet.

The best places to buy carpets are the major shopping malls like City Center Doha and Royal Plaza. To make sure the carpet you are buying is original, ask for a certificate of authenticity. You can get cheaper carpets in the souks but be aware that shop owners are very convincing and will make you believe you are getting a great product at a low price.

### Jewellery & Watches

There are numerous outlets selling watches and jewellery, many of which are in shopping malls. Most major watch brands are available and price tags range from under QR 100 to over QR 100,000. Unsurprisingly for a country that boasts the world's highest per capita income, several high-end jewellers have set up shop in one of Qatar's luxury malls: Lagoona Mall is a particularly good address if big name jewellery is what you're after. Elsewhere, the souks are a great bet for jewellery and watches at various price points. Jewellery is sold by weight and you may find that prices are cheaper here compared to your home country. You will also find plenty of watches on sale in the souks, including some pretty convincing imitations. Every mall will have at least one jeweller, such as the ubiquitous Damas, and of course the Gold Souk is a wall-to-wall wonderland of glittering gold shops. The Gold Souk is located on Ali Bin Abdullah Street and the surrounding area. If you don't see anything you like, it is easy to find a jeweller who will make an item to your specifications. Instances of jewellers conning their customers by selling fake gold at real-gold prices are few and far between; nevertheless it is a good idea to ask for a certificate of authenticity (especially important when buying diamonds). Many stores are clustered around Al Sadd Street as well as the souks, so shop around.

## Souvenirs

Don't fall into the 'my grandma went to Doha and all I got was this lousy T-shirt' souvenir trap; Doha has a wide range of interesting mementos on offer that reflect the special character of Arabia. Souvenirs tend to be similar throughout the GCC countries. Intricately carved wooden trinket boxes, Arabian incense, shisha pipes, fluffy singing camels and miniature brass coffee pots have all found their way into many a suitcase on its way out of the GCC, and Doha is no exception. There are also numerous souvenirs made using sand, the region's most abundant resource, such as pictures and jars holding different coloured sand. Most hotels have little lobby shops that sell a limited range of the standard offerings, but for the best souvenir shopping in Doha head for the souks. Here you'll find wall-to-wall gifts at negotiable prices. There are a few souvenir shops along Abdulla Bin

Thani Street, such as Arts & Crafts, which sells a good range at reasonable prices. Most shopping malls have souvenir shops; and many will also regularly host in-mall exhibitions that showcase the region's favourite types of souvenirs.

## Tailoring & Textiles

As a stopover on major trading routes, the Middle East region has always had a thriving textile market. No matter what colour or type of fabric you are looking for, there are numerous dedicated shops around Doha. Souk Al Dira and Souk Al Asiery have a collection of shops inside air-conditioned buildings, selling all types of fabrics. Tayif Textiles in the Souk Al Asiery is a good place to buy your material, while Lexus Tailors on Al Sadd Street is for men only. Prices tend to be a little more expensive than in individual shops, ranging from QR 30 to QR 800 per yard.

There is no shortage of tailors in Doha and once you find a good one it should be able to make up anything you want. Word of mouth is the best way to find a tailor who is competent and reliable. The tailors in the region can copy any garment, picture or pattern. Head to Al Kahraba Street or Wadi Al Musheirib Street and you will find a good range. Prices don't vary much from one place to another, although highly skilled tailors who can produce more intricate garments, like wedding dresses, are more expensive. Once you have chosen your fabric, you can show your tailor a picture of what you want or even just take in a garment for them to copy.

Shopping

# Going Out

| | |
|---|---|
| **Dining Out** | 168 |
| **Entertainment** | 172 |
| **Venue Directory** | 176 |
| **Area Directory** | 180 |
| **Restaurants & Cafes** | 186 |
| **Nightlife Establishments** | 220 |

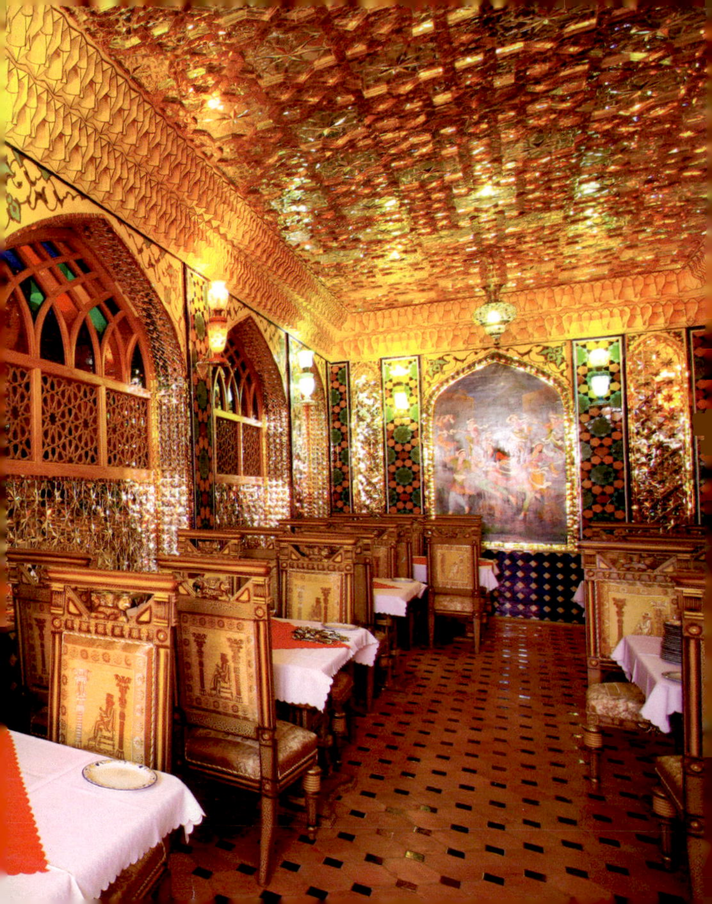

# Dining Out

**Dining out is practically a national pastime in Doha and from celebrity chef-endorsed dining to casual street cafes, visitors are spoilt for choice.**

Although Doha is still a relatively small city, the number of restaurants and entertainment venues is expanding rapidly and visitors will find few issues locating a suitable spot for an evening out – be it a fancy meal, a pint of beer or a bowl of cheap nosh you're after. Five years ago, a business traveller looking for a nightcap would have been limited to a few options in the Radisson Blu, but things are completely different now: while the Radisson Blu is still a nightlife hub, it's no longer the only option when it comes to going out.

All over town, a slew of gorgeous new hotels has raised the culinary bar for travelling gourmands. Restaurants like Megu and Market By Jean-Georges are on a par with any other innovative eatery in the world, and with new hotels springing up all the time – and with multi-billion dollar developments such as The Pearl and the Katara Cultural Village – the choice of what to eat and where to go has never been greater. This said, Qatar's nightlife is concentrated in the capital city; there are currently only a few desirable restaurants or hotels outside Doha. If you're in town on a Friday, be sure to book yourself into one of the big hotel brunches, which are a true Doha institution. Come Friday, all the main hotels offer lavish spreads for a fixed price to make excellent value.

# Eating Out

In Doha, there is a good range of restaurants to choose from, with anything from basic budget canteen-style places to top notch designer dining available. On the whole, prices are on par with most other major cities worldwide and compared with just 10 years ago, the number of restaurants has increased dramatically. Each new hotel usually brings with it a few new options, as do other new developments such as the recently lovingly-renovated Souk Waqif. Thursday and Friday are the busiest nights and it's a good idea to book a table ahead of time if you'd like to sample one of the city's many smart restaurants then. Dining out with the kids is hassle-free: nearly all restaurants are family-friendly. If you have a food allergy – particularly to nuts, which are used a lot – you need to be careful in Doha as menus can be very vague about listing the ingredients. Also, language difficulties, and a general desire to please the customer and say 'yes' to most client requests means that it's best to be careful if you've got special dietary needs.

### Door Policy

The government has introduced new regulations for visitors to hotel clubs, requiring guests to show their passport upon entry. Your ID will be scanned and a membership card printed. Be warned that each hotel has its own card so you may end up carting around a lot of plastic on a night out. Some places charge around QR 100 – 150 for membership.

**Going Out — Dining Out**

## Nightlife

For the moment, apart from a handful of private clubs, the only places that are licensed are the major hotels, which means that you're less likely to be enjoying the kind of night that involves a cheap curry and a pint for a bargain price. You're also not allowed to buy beverages from a licensed store unless you have a licence, which requires, among other things, a Qatar residence visa. That said, you're by no means forced to go empty-handed if you fancy a quick sip to end the day. The major hotels house some very worthwhile nightlife establishments; see the Venue Directory for listings of recommended venues across the city.

## Local Cuisine

Lebanese cuisine is the most commonly exported to the west, but traditional Arabic cuisines vary from country to country. Qatari cuisine is influenced by Indian and Iranian foods; for example, one of the country's signature dishes, machbous, is very similar to the Indian biryani. Most of the Arabic restaurants in Qatar serve a version of Lebanese food, and one of the highlights

**The Yellow Star**
The little yellow star highlights venues that merit extra praise. It could be the atmosphere, the food, the cocktails, the music or the crowd, but whatever the reason, any review that you see with the star attached is somewhere considered a bit special.

is Automatic. Restaurants serving truly authentic, traditional Qatari food are still a rare treat, but luckily there are a few options, including Al Majlis.

## Shisha Cafes

It is common in this part of the world to see men, and some women, of all ages relaxing in the evening with a coffee or juice and a shisha pipe. For visitors and residents, even non-smokers, it's one of those must-do experiences and could just become a regular pastime. Many of the Arabic cafes and restaurants around town have shisha available and it makes a perfect end to a meal, especially when sitting outdoors – try Al Wanis Shisha Terrace (4425 6666) at Sharq Village and Spa for a beautiful alfresco spot with great views to boot. If you fancy buying your own for a souvenir, then the souks are a good place to start your search, but most souvenir shops sell shisha pipes, as do the larger supermarkets.

> **Vegetarian Food**
> Meat plays heavily in Arabic mains, but many of the appetisers, such as hummus, baba ganoush and the various salads, are vegetarian. Also, many of the American or European chain restaurants are used to catering to non-meat eaters and will always have a vegetarian option on the menu. There are plenty of independent Indian restaurants that serve only vegetarian food, often very cheaply.

# Entertainment

**Qatar's live entertainment scene may be in its infancy, but that doesn't mean there isn't plenty of choice to keep you busy.**

## Cinema

A trip to the cinema is among the most popular ways to spend an evening out on these shores. Unlike as recently as five years ago, today's Doha has plenty of cinemas, and with the openings of the Villaggio cinema in 2009 and The Pearl's IMAX cinema in 2014, movie-goers have even more choice. Almost all the major releases are shown in theatres across Doha, usually at the same time as in other major cities worldwide. However, it's worthwhile to know that movies with what is considered 'unsuitable' content may be shown in an edited format. Major international Hollywood blockbusters aside, there is also a big market for Arab and Indian films. For movie listings, grab a copy of one of the local papers.

## Comedy

In addition to regular Laughter Factory nights at the Radisson Blu (see below), amateur theatre group Doha Players (5575 5102) sometimes holds cabaret nights for its members.

### The Laughter Factory
thelaughterfactory.com                                   4441 7417

The Laughter Factory, a company that brings international comedians to the Gulf, comes to Doha once a month for two nights when three stand-up comics try to avoid the hecklers and get maximum laughs. The standard is usually pretty good and while most of the comics are British, you get a few other nationalities too. The shows take place in the Radisson Blu (4428 1428) and often sell out, so get your tickets in advance from the hotel. Entry is QR 90 and shows start at 8pm. Simple meals are available before the acts come on stage to make this a good option for an evening out.

## Concerts & Live Music

The Katara Cultural Village in West Bay has a huge open-air style amphitheatre that sometimes hosts opera and ballet productions; there is also a smaller indoor theatre that stages productions. In the past, relatively few big-ticket international entertainers have made their way to Doha during their world tours, but the Doha

**Connected Venues**
Whether you want to go online while enjoying a coffee or having a bite to eat, many restaurants and cafes now offer internet connection for their customers. In addition, Ooredoo's network of wireless hotspots at hotels, restaurants and coffee shops is constantly growing. Current locations include the InterContinental Hotel, the Merweb Hotel, both branches of Eli France (Salwa and City Center Doha), La Maison du Cafe (Salwa and Royal Plaza Mall), Le Notre, Grand Cafe, Crepaway and Fauchon. For complete listings and more details on the service, see Ooredoo.com.

Film Festival usually attracts a number of A-list celebrities and the annual Big Day Out music concert in 2011 brought over a couple of American chart-toppers. The big hotels also occasionally stage concerts, as does the National Theatre. If you fancy a cultural experience during your stay, your best bets are to check with your hotel's concierge and keep an eye out on listings in local media and publications listed.

## Fashion Shows

As a country that's home to an ever-growing number of designer boutiques, Qatar is certainly a fashion-conscious corner of the world. Shopping aside, fashionistas who've found themselves here get to enjoy a fashion shows that are sporadically held during the year by various non-profit organisations such as the American Womens' Association (awaqatar.com) and Virginia Commonwealth University's School of Fashion Design (qatar.vcu.edu).

## Theatre

The best-known theatrical company in Qatar is the Doha Players. Made up of talented amateurs and volunteers, the group has been staging English-language productions for over 50 years. It no longer has its own theatre, but the company has raised funds and is now drawing up plans for a new venue. In the meantime, the Doha Players has been using various venues around the capital, including Doha Sailing Club and, for bigger productions like the annual pantomime and musicals, the College of the North Atlantic.

Entertainment **Going Out**

**Going Out**

# Venue Directory

## Cafes & Restaurants

**American**

| | | |
|---|---|---|
| | American Grill | p.191 |
| | Fuddruckers | p.195 |
| | Johnny Rockets | p.198 |
| | Ponderosa | p.206 |

**Arabic**

| | | |
|---|---|---|
| | Al Hamra | p.182 |
| | Al Khaima | p.183 |
| | Al Liwan | p.183 |
| | Al Majlis | p.184 |
| | Al Mourjan | p.184 |
| | Albatross | p.186 |
| | Albisana Kunafa | p.186 |
| | Assaha Lebanese Traditional Village | p.188 |
| | Automatic | p.188 |
| | Beirut Restaurant | p.189 |
| | Burj Al Haman | p.190 |
| | ⭐ Layali Restaurant | p.200 |
| | Shawarma Albisana | p.208 |
| | Shisha Garden | p.208 |
| | The Tent | p.212 |

**Cafes & Coffee Shops**

| | | |
|---|---|---|
| | ⭐ Alison Nelson's Chocolate Bar | p.186 |
| | Cafe Amici | p.190 |
| | Gourmet House | p.196 |
| | J&G Sandwich Cellar | p.198 |
| | Lobby Lounge | p.202 |
| | Orangery Cafe Trottoir | p.204 |
| | The Lobby Lounge | p.202 |

Qatar **Visitors'** Guide

**Chinese**

| | |
|---|---|
| Beijing | p.188 |
| Chopsticks | p.192 |
| Hakkasan | p.199 |
| Tse Yang | p.214 |

**European**

| | |
|---|---|
| Aroma | p.187 |

**Far Eastern**

| | |
|---|---|
| Asia Live! | p.187 |
| Thai Noodles | p.214 |

**French**

| | |
|---|---|
| Fauchon | p.194 |
| La Mer | p.199 |

**Indian**

| | |
|---|---|
| Taj Rasoi | p.211 |
| The Garden Restaurant | p.195 |

**International**

| | |
|---|---|
| Al Hasbah | p.187 |
| Bistro 61 | p.189 |
| Blue | p.189 |
| Cafe Bateel | p.190 |
| Cosmo | p.193 |
| Crepaway | p.193 |
| Flavours | p.195 |
| Fork & Knife | p.218 |
| Le Cigalon Restaurant | p.201 |
| Market by Jean-Georges | p.202 |
| Neo Restaurant | p.203 |
| Opal by Gordon Ramsay | p.204 |
| Richoux | p.207 |

Going Out

Venue Directory

## Venue Directory — Going Out

|  |  |  |
|---|---|---|
|  | The Lagoon | p.200 |
|  | The Square | p.210 |
|  | Victoria | p.215 |
| **Italian** |  |  |
|  | American Grill | p.191 |
|  | Ciao | p.192 |
|  | Di Capri | p.194 |
|  | Il Teatro | p.196 |
|  | Porcini | p.206 |
|  | Trattoria | p.218 |
| **Japanese** |  |  |
|  | Megu | p.203 |
|  | Yen Sushi Bar | p.215 |
| **Mediterranean** |  |  |
|  | Corniche | p.192 |
|  | La Villa | p.199 |
|  | Le Central Restaurant | p.201 |
|  | Seasons Restaurant | p.208 |
| **Mexican** |  |  |
|  | Salsa | p.207 |
| **Moroccan** |  |  |
|  | Tajine | p.212 |
|  | Tangia | p.212 |
| **Seafood** |  |  |
|  | Al Dana | p.182 |
|  | Al Sayyad | p.184 |
|  | L'Wzaar Seafood Restaurant | p.199 |
|  | Strata | p.211 |
|  | The Fish Market | p.194 |

**South-East Asian**

| | Spice Market | p.210 |

**Steakhouse**

| | JW's Steakhouse | p.198 |
| | The Old Manor | p.203 |

**Tex Mex**

| | Paloma | p.204 |

**Turkish**

| | Sukar Pasha Ottoman Lounge | p.211 |

# Nightlife Establishments

| | Admiral's Club | p.216 |
| | Cigar Lounge | p.216 |
| | Crystal | p.216 |
| | Habanos | p.217 |
| | Hive | p.217 |
| | Jazz At The Lincoln | p.222 |
| | Jazz Up Bar | p.218 |
| | Lava | p.218 |
| | The Library Bar & Cigar Lounge | p.219 |
| | The Lounge | p.219 |
| | Pearl Lounge Club | p.219 |
| | Qube | p.220 |
| | Seven | p.220 |
| | Wahm | p.200 |

askexplorer.com

# Area Directory — Going Out

## Al Dafna, Al Gassar & West Bay

### Restaurant

| | | |
|---|---|---|
| Al Hasbah | Dana Club | p.187 |
| Al Sayyad | The Diplomatic Club | p.184 |
| American Grill | Somerst Tower Hotel | p.191 |
| Aroma | Kempinski Residences & Suites, Doha | p.187 |
| Bistro 61 | Al Fardan Towers | p.189 |
| Cafe Amici | City Center Doha | p.190 |
| Fork & Knife House | Mövenpick Tower & Suites Doha | p.215 |
| Gourmet House | Kempinski Residences & Suites, Doha | p.196 |
| Hakkasan | St Regis Doha | p.199 |
| Hwang | InterContinental Doha | p.200 |
| Il Teatro | Four Seasons Hotel | p.196 |
| La Mer | The Ritz-Carlton Doha | p.199 |
| Market by Jean-Georges | W Doha Hotel & Residences | p.202 |
| Mawasem | Hilton Doha | p.206 |
| Paloma | InterContinental Doha | p.204 |
| Prime | InterContinental Doha | p.210 |
| Porcini | The Ritz-Carlton Doha | p.206 |
| Richoux | City Center Doha | p.207 |
| Spice Market | W Doha Hotel & Residences | p.210 |
| The Fish Market | InterContinental Doha | p.194 |
| The Lagoon | The Ritz-Carlton Doha | p.200 |
| Trader Vic's | Hilton Doha | p.218 |

**Nightlife**

| | | |
|---|---|---|
| Admiral's Club | The Ritz-Carlton Doha | p.216 |
| Crystal | W Doha Hotel & Residences | p.216 |
| Habanos | The Ritz-Carlton Doha | p.217 |
| Jazz At The Lincoln | St Regis Doha | p.222 |
| The Library Bar & Cigar Lounge | Four Seasons Hotel | p.219 |
| The Lounge | Kempinski Residences & Suites, Doha | p.219 |
| Wahm | W Doha Hotel & Residences | p.220 |

## Al Gassar
**Restaurant**

| | | |
|---|---|---|
| Albisana Kunafa | Katara Cultural Village | p.186 |
| Astor Grill | St Regis Doha | p.192 |
| L'Wzaar Seafood Restaurant | Katara Cultural Village | p.199 |
| Opal by Gordon Ramsay | St Regis Doha | p.204 |
| Shawarma Albisana | Katara Cultural Village | p.208 |
| Sukar Pasha Ottoman Lounge | Katara Cultural Village | p.211 |
| The Lobby Lounge | The Ritz-Carlton Doha | p.202 |

**Nightlife**

| | | |
|---|---|---|
| Lava | InterContinental Doha | p.218 |

## Al Khulaifat
**Restaurant**

| | | |
|---|---|---|
| Al Dana | Sharq Village & Spa | p.182 |
| JW's Steakhouse | Doha Marriott Hotel | p.198 |

## Al Sadd & Al Rayyan Road
**Restaurant**

| | | |
|---|---|---|
| Al Hamra | Al Rayyan Complex | p.182 |
| Al Khaima | Al Sadd Rd | p.183 |
| Al Majlis | Al Sadd Rd | p.184 |
| Automatic | Al Sadd Rd | p.188 |
| Chopsticks | Wyndham Grand Regency Doha | p.192 |
| Cosmo | Millennium Hotel Doha | p.193 |
| Le Central Restaurant | La Cigale Hotel | p.201 |
| Le Cigalon Restaurant | La Cigale Hotel | p.201 |
| Star of India | Khalifa St | p.210 |
| Tangia | Wyndham Grand Regency Doha | p.212 |
| Yen Sushi Bar | La Cigale Hotel | p.214 |

**Nightlife**

| | | |
|---|---|---|
| Seven | La Cigale Hotel | p.220 |

## Baaya
**Restaurant**

| | | |
|---|---|---|
| Blue | Grand Heritage Doha Hotel & Spa | p.189 |

| | | |
|---|---|---|
| Flavours | Grand Heritage Doha Hotel & Spa | p.195 |
| Victoria | Grand Heritage Doha Hotel & Spa | p.215 |

## Doha Corniche
**Restaurant**

| | | |
|---|---|---|
| Al Mourjan | The Corniche | p.184 |
| Beirut Restaurant | Al Kahraba St | p.189 |

## Fereej Bin Mahmoud
**Restaurant**

| | | |
|---|---|---|
| Di Capri | La Cigale Hotel | p.194 |
| Orangery Cafe Trottoir | La Cigale Hotel | p.204 |
| Shisha Garden | La Cigale Hotel | p.208 |

## Khalifa Street & Al Luqta Street
**Restaurant**

| | | |
|---|---|---|
| Fuddruckers | Khalifa International Tennis & Squash Complex | p.195 |

## Onaiza
**Nightlife**

| | | |
|---|---|---|
| Hive | InterContinental Doha The City | p.217 |

**Restaurant**

| | | |
|---|---|---|
| Lobby Lounge | InterContinental Doha The City | p.202 |
| Strata | InterContinental Doha The City | p.211 |

Going Out

Venue Directory

| | | |
|---|---|---|
| Square | InterContinental Doha The City | p.210 |

## Salwa Road & Al Aziziya
**Restaurant**

| | | |
|---|---|---|
| Beijing | Off Salwa Rd | p.188 |
| Cafe Bateel | Salwa Rd | p.190 |
| Ciao | Haya Complex | p.192 |
| Crepaway | Al Mouthanna Complex | p.193 |
| Fauchon | Souq Najad | p.194 |
| Johnny Rockets | Al Emadi Centre | p.198 |
| Layali Restaurant | Souq Najad | p.200 |
| Neo Restaurant | Souq Najad | p.203 |
| Ponderosa | Salwa Rd | p.206 |

**Nightlife**

| | | |
|---|---|---|
| Qube | Radisson Blu Hotel, Doha | p.220 |

## Slata
**Nightlife**

| | | |
|---|---|---|
| Jazz Up Bar | Mövenpick Hotel Doha | p.218 |

## Souk Area & Souk Waqif
**Restaurant**

| | | |
|---|---|---|
| Al Liwan | Sharq Village & Spa | p.183 |
| Albatross | Al Bustan Hotel | p.186 |
| Asia Live! | Doha Marriott Hotel | p.187 |

| | | |
|---|---|---|
| Assaha Lebanese Traditional Village | Hamad Al Kibir St | p.188 |
| Corniche | Doha Marriott Hotel | p.192 |
| J&G Sandwich Cellar | Ras Abu Aboud St | p.198 |
| La Villa | Mercure Grand Hotel Doha City Centre | p.199 |
| Salsa | Doha Marriott Hotel | p.207 |
| Seasons Restaurant | Mövenpick Hotel Doha | p.208 |
| Taj Rasoi | Doha Marriott Hotel | p.211 |
| Tajine | Souk Waqif | p.212 |
| Thai Noodles | Al Mahmal St | p.214 |
| The Garden | Najma St | p.195 |
| The Old Manor | Mercure Grand Hotel Doha City Centre | p.203 |
| The Tent | Al Bustan Hotel | p.212 |
| Trattoria | Concorde Hotel | p.218 |

**Nightlife**

| | | |
|---|---|---|
| Cigar Lounge | Sharq Village & Spa | p.216 |
| The Pearl Lounge Club | Doha Marriott Hotel | p.219 |

# The Pearl
**Restaurant**

| | | |
|---|---|---|
| Alison Nelson's Chocolate Bar | Porto Arabia | p.186 |
| Burj Al Haman | Porto Arabia | p.190 |
| Megu | Porto Arabia | p.203 |
| Tse Yang | Porto Arabia | p.214 |

## Restaurants & Cafes

Dining out is a national pastime in Doha and from celebrity chef haunts to casual street cafes, visitors are spoilt for choice when it comes to eating options.

### Al Dana
Sharq Village & Spa, Al Khulaifat

Seafood
4425 6666

The airy, open spaces in Al Dana revolve around a beautifully laid-out fish counter in the centre of the room. Most of the fish on display are fresh from the Gulf. The restaurant is covered in flashes of blue and turquoise. Diners can select a fish of their choice and preparation method, order from the sushi menu, or pick and choose from the extensive a la carte selection. The best bet is to stick to the sushi and fresh fish options for your main course – this is the area where Al Dana truly excels. **Map** 1 K5

### Al Hamra
Al Rayyan Complex, Al Rayyan Rd, Musheireb

Arabic
4443 3297

Al Hamra offers casual dining with a full Arabic menu, making it a great place to stop by for a quick bite that will also serve as an introduction to Arabian eating. Located close to the souks (behind Al Reem Pharmacy), it's also a good bet for shoppers in need of a break. In this case, the selection of fresh juices on offer here is a fabulous way to boost your energy levels. This is also a good spot for breakfast, with the thyme-flavoured breads (zaatar) and traditional mint tea both recommended. **Map** 1 G4

### Al Hasbah

International

Dana Club, Al Dafna                                          4496 0600

Casual yet charming, Al Hasbah serves a delicious mix of Mediterranean and International cuisine meaning there is something to suit everyone's taste buds. The family-friendly setting is both stylish and comfortable. Try the Caesar salad and the homemade ginger lemonade. With generous servings, don't be shy to ask for a takeaway. **Map** 1 G3

### Al Khaima

Arabic

Nr Asmakh Mall, Al Sadd Rd, Al Sadd                4444 6962

Al Khaima literally translated means 'the tent', and diners here can relax in traditional tented surroundings around the clock as the restaurant is open 24 hours. Known for its quality Arabian cuisine, the restaurant serves each dish with a side order of fresh, oval-shaped bread. The tasty food is hard to resist, so it's a good idea to arrive hungry. This is also a great venue for families with children. **Map** 1 E5

### Al Liwan

Arabic

Sharq Village & Spa, Al Khulaifat                        4425 6666

Not just your average buffet, Al Liwan offers an extensive array of tasty Qatari and Arabic cuisine. Start with hot and cold Lebanese mezze, salads and bread straight from the oven. The fresh seafood and koftas (meatballs) are particularly good and regional main courses change regularly. The samak chermoula – kingfish with pomegranate couscous – is delicious. Those with a sweet tooth will love the well-stocked dessert station. **Map** 1 K5

### Al Majlis — Arabic
Nr Asmakh Mall, Al Sadd Rd, Al Sadd — 4444 7417

This popular restaurant is known for its authentic dining experience. The upstairs level has intimate cubicles with curtains, while downstairs you can dine seated on Arabic cushions and carpets. The traditional Arabic menu features mezze and grilled meats, as well as the signature hammour fish with baby shrimp and cheese. **Map** 1 E5

### Al Mourjan — Arabic
The Corniche, Al Dafna — 4483 4423

Whether you dine indoors in the immaculate white furnished dining area or outside enjoying the gentle breezes coming off the Corniche, a visit to Al Mourjan is a wonderful way to pass an evening as you linger over a vast Lebanese spread so big that it may not all fit on your table at once. The terrace seating offers views of the Corniche all the way to the Islamic museum in one direction and the Sheraton in the other. After dinner, you can choose from no fewer than 300 shisha pipes for a smoke under the stars. **Map** 1 G3

### Al Sayyad — Seafood
The Diplomatic Club, Al Gassar — 4484 7444

This established restaurant is a good choice for a relaxing night out. Set just off the beach at the Diplomatic Club, with outside seating for the cooler months, it offers a great choice of seafood. Sit back and enjoy the authentic Arabic salads while you take your pick from the menu. If you can't decide, the waiters are on hand with helpful advice. **Map** 3 D2

Going Out

**Going Out**

**Restaurants & Cafes**

### Albatross Restaurant
Al Bustan Hotel, Slata

Arabic
4432 8888

This pleasant all-rounder restaurant is popular with local families and it's not hard to see why. The menu is international but with a definite Lebanese accent, meaning there is something for everyone. The generous portions are beautifully prepared and presented; and served in a relaxed atmosphere by friendly and knowledgeable staff. **Map** 1 J4

### Albisana Kunafa
Katara Cultural Village, Al Gassar

Arabic
4408 1200

A honeyed taste of Palestine and Jordan is on offer at Albisana Kunafa. The bistro-style venue specialises in two iconic Middle Eastern desserts, kunafa and mohalibya. The former is served hot and created using a traditional Palestinian recipe, which features Nabulsi cheese, honey and a sprinkling of pistachio. Mohalibya, a milky jelly with seductive flavours of honey and rose water, is served cold as a perfect summer treat. **Map** 3 D2

### Alison Nelson's Chocolate Bar   Cafes & Coffee Shops
Porto Arabia, The Pearl

4495 3878

Everything from the Chocolate Bar's decor to the menu is innovative and intentionally cool. You can choose to relax inside on the club lounge's pristine white sofas, or opt for the outdoors garden chairs for an alfresco experience. Either way, be prepared for a chocoholic's dream come true: chocolate is woven cleverly throughout the menu.
**Map** 3 D2

## American Grill
American
4411 0188
Somerset Tower, Al Gassar

An unpretentious but well-presented venue for breakfast, lunch or dinner. Choose from an appetising pancake to get you through until lunch. For lunch or dinner, choose a grilled chicken or steak dish and a healthy salad at this unassuming restaurant. This a great spot for a family meal out because there is something for everybody on this extensive menu.
**Map** 3 D2

## Aroma
European
4405 3325
Kempinski Residences & Suites, Doha, Al Dafna

This all-day dining haunt serves modern European food in a classy, low-key setting that's equally suited for business lunches or a quiet dinner-a-deux. The brasserie-style starters and mains come in generous portions, and the clean decor lets the great quality of the international food do the talking. A mouthwatering dessert menu completes the experience.
**Map** 1 H1

## Asia Live!
Far Eastern
4429 8472
Doha Marriott Hotel, Al Khulaifat

Asia Live's popularity is partly due to the two teppanyaki cooking stations that let diners get up close to the furious slapping, chopping, throwing and catching of their soon-to-be meals. There is also a sushi bar on hand, as well as an a la carte menu. Fortunately for the romantics, the dark-wood decor and interesting layout also allows for semi-private dinners. **Map** 1 K4

## Restaurants & Cafes

### Assaha Lebanese Traditional Village
Arabic
Hamad Al Kibir St, Al Doha Al Jadeeda    4435 5353

Set in a lovely stone building, this Lebanese restaurant is designed to feel like an old village. Despite its large size, the interior feels cosy thanks to the private rooms and nooks and crannies. The grilled meats and traditional mezze are delicious, and the bread is even better. To get here, go up Grand Hamad Street from the Corniche, cross the A Ring Road and make your way another 200m on the right past Olympic Sports.
**Map** 1 H5

### Astor Grill At St Regis
Steakhouse
St Regis Doha, Al Gassar    4446 0211

This restaurant is designed in the style of a classic New York steakhouse and grill, and it serves fresh seafood and top quality beef from its charcoal grill. You'll also find classics such as Waldorf salad, Oysters Rockefeller and sumptuous New York cheesecake. The menu changes regularly and is good for both foodies and busy business travellers. You can book the Chef's Table for the best view of the chef at work.  **Map** 3 D2

### Automatic
Arabic
Nr Al Muftah Centre, Al Sadd Rd, Al Sadd    4442 5999

This small chain of restaurants has been serving great quality Arabic food in a casual setting across the Middle East for years. The menu sports a good selection of inexpensive mezzes and salads as well as grilled meat, fish and kebabs. It's also a great option for grabbing a morning pastry and coffee before hitting the sights.  **Map** 1 E5

### Beijing
Chinese

Nr The Centre, Off Salwa Rd, Fereej Abdel Aziz　　4435 8688

This independent restaurant is nestled in a private villa off the busy Salwa Road. It has both indoor and outdoor seating, which is suitable for large groups, as well as more intimate private dining areas separated by cubicles. Beijing has friendly, knowledgeable staff who can help you choose from the extensive menu, which features a good selection of great tasting traditional Chinese favourites. They are big on portions, so be prepared to unbuckle your belt. **Map** 1 F5

### Beirut Restaurant
Arabic

Al Kahraba St, Fereej Mohd Bin Jasim　　4442 1087

Feel like a local by pulling your car up to the front door of this predominantly takeaway restaurant. Soon enough, a waiter will run out to your car window to take your order. Serving a good selection of Lebanese food, Beirut is known to many residents for its fabulous hummus and foul, a traditional bean dish popular throughout the Arab world. **Map** 1 H4

### Bistro 61
International

Al Fardan Towers, 61 Al Funduq St, Al Dafna　　4498 9393

This West Bay cafe-restaurant features Elizabethan-style furnishings, ornate chandeliers and an ultra-modern glass ceiling to make an airy, quirky setting. The menu is among the most varied in town: scrumptious starters, pizzas, sandwiches and grilled mains, as well as an impressive list of hot beverages, smoothies and juices is on offer. It's a popular spot for residents living in the nearby towers. **Map** 1 G2

## Restaurants & Cafes — Going Out

### Blue
**International**
Grand Heritage Doha Hotel & Spa, Baaya
4445 5555

A bit of an underappreciated gem in Doha's fine dining scene, Blue offers an array of international culinary delights: in addition to some of the best sushi in town, the menu ranges from the likes of pumpkin curry soup to superb steaks. The desserts are also worth a try, particularly the signature cheesecake which comes with delightfully a local kick as it's made of dates. Impeccable presentation and friendly service complete the picture. **Map** 3 A5

### Burj Al Hamam
**Arabic**
Porto Arabia, The Pearl
4495 3876

This is a fine choice for a taste of high-end Lebanese cuisine. The restaurant offers incredible views of the marina as you dine inside a stunningly spacious room clad with chandeliers, white pillars and modern furniture. The food is an impressive array of traditional Lebanese treats including cold mezze plates of hummus, moutabal, tabouli and fragrant, flavourful grilled lamb and shish kebab. **Map** 3 D2

### Cafe Amici
**Cafes & Coffee Shops**
City Center Doha, Al Dafna
4483 4811

In the midst of the jewellery shops at the far end of City Center, Cafe Amici is a haven of calm. The biggest draw has to be the comfy armchairs where you can take the weight off your feet and forget about shopping for a while. The staff are great and there is a good selection of croissants, sandwiches and cakes, making it perfect for afternoon tea. **Map** 1 H1

*Clockwise from top left: Le Cigalon, Le Central, Astor Grill At St Regis*

Going Out

## Cafe Bateel
International

Nr Midmac Interchange, Salwa Rd, Fereej Al Nasr   4444 1414

As you head out of Doha on Salwa Road, Cafe Bateel is easy to miss, but worth seeking out. Menu options include superb salads, soups and sandwiches, plus heartier main courses that take cues from India, Italy and Arabia. The interior features wooden alcoves, Arabic cushions and barasti palm ceilings. Upstairs is the family room, as well as a games room where the kids will be entertained for hours.  **Map** 1 E6

## Chopsticks
Chinese

Wyndham Grand Regency Doha, Al Sadd   4434 3333

In a pleasant setting befitting this smart hotel, Chopsticks is on the lobby level of the Grand Regency. The restaurant serves all the usual favourites from the orient, expertly prepared in an authentic style. The menu features a good selection of rice and noodle dishes, suitable for both vegetarians and meat-eaters. The restaurant is open for both lunch and dinner; however, it's an unlicensed venue so alcohol is not available.  **Map** 1 E4

## Ciao
Italian

Haya Complex, Salwa Rd, Fereej Al Soudan   4468 9100

This centrally located independent restaurant goes the extra mile to provide a true taste of Italia, right down to having its cheeses specially flown in. The pizzas and calzones are cooked in an open oven on the main level of the restaurant. When it comes to desserts, the tiramisu cannot be missed, although it faces stiff competition from the gelato.  **Map** 3 C5

### Corniche
Doha Marriott Hotel, Al Khulaifat — Mediterranean — 4429 8404

This is one of the biggest all-you-can-eat buffets in Qatar, with a varied selection of freshly prepared dishes from across the globe. The speciality would have to be the seafood bonanza available every evening from 7pm. The setting is impressive too – it's a light and airy conservatory with views of the pool and gardens. The Friday brunch is popular, with a hugely diverse range of dishes and entertainment for children. **Map** 1 K4

### Cosmo
Millennium Hotel Doha, Al Sadd — International — 4424 7777

This large restaurant on the ground floor of the Millennium Hotel offers daily lunch and dinner brunch deals. Millennium is dry making it popular with Arabic clientele. There is an ample selection of international fare. The sober ambience makes it a good choice for a meal with business associates; just be sure to arrive at the beginning of a sitting as the dishes tend to run out later on. **Map** 1 E5

### Crepaway
Al Mouthanna Complex, Salwa Rd, Al Mirqab — International — 4465 5830

As the name suggests, the menu here features a large, lip-smacking selection of sweet and savoury crepes. Open for breakfast, lunch and dinner, it also serves salads, sandwiches, pizzas, pastas and desserts. The good food is matched by the good mood, and the jukebox and live DJ produce the feel of a fun, young and upbeat diner. **Map** 1 F6

## Di Capri

*Italian*

La Cigale Hotel, Fereej Bin Mahmoud  4428 8888

This Italian offers a quirky mixture of modern and traditional, evident in both the decor and the food. The menu is inspired by the famous resort island of Capri and features a selection of fresh salads: the Caprese Salad in particular is not to be missed. Homemade pasta dishes, risottos and some hearty meat and seafood options are also available. There's no separate kids' menu, but adaptations are available on request. **Map** 1 F5

## Fauchon

*French*

Souq Najad, Salwa Rd, New Al Mirqab  4432 4888

Although it markets itself as a specialist tea house, Fauchon serves a wide range of fine Gallic culinary treats for those with a sweet tooth. As well as impeccably brewed gourmet teas, full-flavoured coffee and superb pastries are served: in fact, it can safely be said that Fauchon dishes up some of the most decadent desserts in the city. **Map** 1 F6

## The Fish Market

*Seafood*

InterContinental Doha, Al Gassar  4484 4444

Instead of reading the menu, pick your fresh fish and vegetables from market-style displays and have the chef cook it however you like. Some people love this, but others prefer not to eyeball their fish on the ice before eating it. The restaurant is in a great setting on the edge of the beach. For a romantic evening in the cooler months, sit on the covered terrace and enjoy the sea views and starry sky. **Map** 3 D2

### Flavours
Grand Heritage Doha Hotel & Spa, Baaya  
International  
4445 5555

This all-day dining restaurant's comfy upholstered seats make it a pleasant, relaxed venue for business meetings or family get-togethers. The restaurant's ample buffet offers food from around the world, with an excellent Arabic mezze section, unusual salads and delicious flavoured breads – particularly the olive and tomato kinds – being the highlights. You can also opt for steak dishes or locally-caught seafood, both cooked to order in the open kitchen. **Map** 3 A5

### Fuddruckers
Khalifa International Tennis & Squash Complex  
American  
4483 3983

Children are provided with an elaborate play space outside, allowing the grown-ups some relative peace and quiet in the Americana themed dining area. Portions are massive and Fuddruckers particularly prides itself on its steaks and burgers. Wash it all down with bottomless sodas and shakes. **Map** 1 F2

### Hakkasan
St Regis Doha, Al Gassar  
Chinese  
4446 0170

This award-winning restaurant deserves all the credit it has garnered since opening in 2013. The exquisite menu is a delight of Cantonese specialities, all cooked to perfection. Hakkasan's signature dishes are its sumptuous stir-fries, such as winged-bean duck and Shanghai lamb tenderloin. Celebrate a special occasion or head over one Friday to enjoy their weekly dim-sum lunches. **Map** 1 D2

## Restaurants & Cafes

### The Garden Restaurant
Indian
Al Najma Souq, Najma  4436 5686

With cheap but well-made curry, The Garden is cleverly split into separate dining areas: downstairs for vegetarian dishes, and upstairs for a la carte or buffet style dining. Rich reds and golds are abundant and there is a choice of open tables and private booths. The waiters are full of smiles, and if you're a fan of Indian food, chances you'll be smiling too. **Map** 1 H6

### Gourmet House
Cafes & Coffee Shops
Kempinski Residences & Suites, Doha, Al Dafna  4405 3326

Authentic, European-style bread makes Gourmet House a firm favourite among Doha expats. The in-house baker is Dutch and some of the specialities include deliciously dark rye bread and soft pretzels. A superb assortment of pastries, pies and cakes, as well as a small selection of sandwiches and delicatessen items, are also available for takeaway or consumption on the spot. **Map** 1 H1

### Hwang
Asian
InterContinental Doha The City, West Bay  4015 8888

Casual yet refined, this pan-Asian restaurant is getting glowing reviews. Cuisine is from Thailand, Korea, Japan, China, the Philippines, Singapore, Indonesia and Malaysia. Try their shabu-shabu, which blends Asian and Middle Eastern flavours – it's perfect for sharing. The staff are very friendly, and more than willing to go the extra mile to make birthdays or anniversaries even more special. **Map** 1 G2

**Going Out**

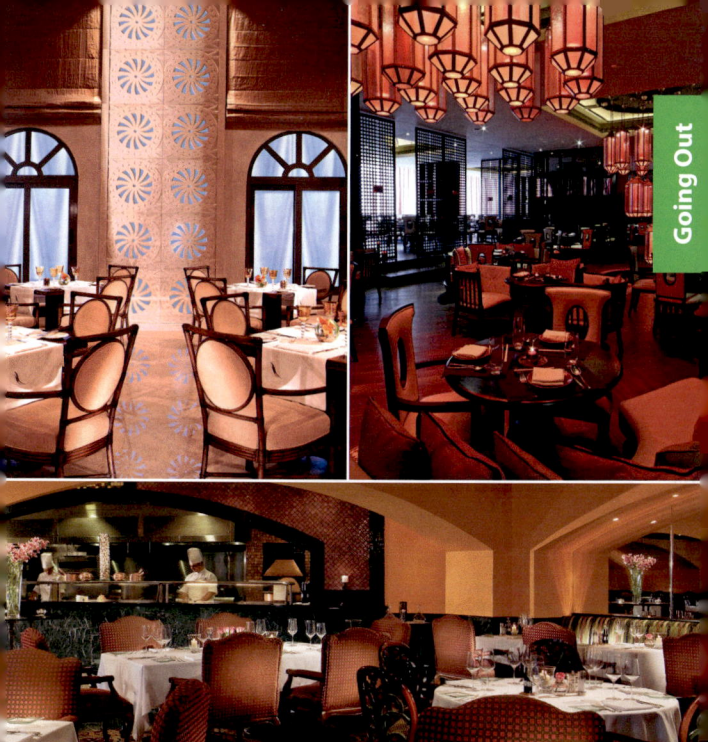

### Il Teatro

Italian
Four Seasons Hotel, Al Dafna  4494 8888

The glass-encased wine cellar and harpist are clear signs that Il Teatro strives to impress. Glass sculptures splash the room with colour, while marble floors and wood trim create a subdued atmosphere. The food is modern Italian and might just be the best in Doha. Even on the busiest nights, the attentive waiting staff seem to anticipate your every move. The all-Italian wine list offers good variety. **Map** 1 H1

### J&G Sandwich Cellar

Cafes & Coffee Shops
Ras Abu Aboud Rd, Al Khulaifat  4435 7559

This is a popular English-owned cafe that serves traditional English food – and for some Brits it may feel like they have walked straight into their mother's kitchen. J&G Sandwich Cellar is a good place for a dose of comfort food and to catch up on newspapers from home. Good sandwiches are available and you can buy food to take away. **Map** 1 K5

### Johnny Rockets

American
Al Emadi Centre, Salwa Rd, New Al Mirqab  4455 2792

Johnny Rockets attempts to recreate the atmosphere of a classic American diner, complete with colourful 1950s-style booths and enthusiastic singing staff (put *YMCA* on the jukebox and see what happens). The menu is loaded with traditional favourites including burgers, hot dogs, chicken dishes and thick milkshakes. Between 7am and 1pm the restaurant offers a full breakfast menu featuring such delights as French toast and pancakes. **Map** 1 F6

### JW's Steakhouse
**Doha Marriott Hotel, Al Khulaifat**
Steakhouse
4429 8499

The Wild West meets a refined gentleman's club in this lively saloon, where hearty steaks and good service are the norm. Novelties include huge chalkboard menus, the braces-clad staff and bullhorn-edged serving boards. Stop by for a beverage with friends and try a fresh US-certified Angus steak to cure a carnivorous craving. **Map** 1 K4

### L'Wzaar Seafood Restaurant
**Katara Cultural Village, Al Gassar**
Seafood
4408 0711

Buzzing, colourful and unashamedly flashy, L'Wzaar is a favourite among the in-crowd. Yet the atmosphere is pleasantly casual and the prices reasonable – in short, if you're looking for a seafront spot with friendly service and fantastically fresh fish, this is it. The food selection is enormous, ranging from fish and chips to sashimi. There are three restaurant sections and, although the place is huge, it fills up every night so book ahead. **Map** 3 D2

### La Mer
**The Ritz-Carlton Doha, Al Gassar**
French
4484 8000

On the top floor of the Ritz-Carlton, La Mer has exceptional views of Doha's waterfront and The Pearl development. This is a classy joint, with gleaming silverware, fine china, sparkling chandeliers and faultless French cuisine – it's surely a contender for the ultimate dining experience in Qatar. The restaurant's layout is perfect for both a pre-dinner beverage or a full-blown dining experience. **Map** 3 D1

*Going Out — Restaurants & Cafes*

**Restaurants & Cafes — Going Out**

### La Villa
Mediterranean
Mercure Grand Hotel Doha City Centre, Al Jasra   4446 2222

This spacious modern restaurant is on the 12th floor of the Mercure Grand in the heart of the city. The choice of dishes is good and some are prepared with an unexpected twist. All are creatively presented. The service is friendly and there are great views of the bustling city below the Doha skyline and the view towards West Bay is lovely.
**Map** 1 G5

### The Lagoon
International
The Ritz-Carlton Doha, Al Gassar   4484 8000

Open all day and bursting at the seams with choices, the temptation here is to try it all. With live cooking stations, the talented chefs will prepare select dishes freshly to order. As you would expect from the Ritz-Carlton, the food is beautifully presented and the service is impeccable, with staff super-keen to please. The Friday brunch is particularly popular, especially with families.  **Map** 3 D1

### Layali Restaurant
Arabic
Souq Najad, Salwa Rd, New Al Mirqab   4431 0005

If you are looking for a truly authentic Lebanese experience, then Layali is a must. The food is impeccable and the staff, in their smart black uniforms, are polished and extremely attentive. Many people go for the wide selection of Arabic mezzes, either hot or cold, but the grilled meats and fish are the real stars. Layali is also known to have some of the best shisha in town.  **Map** 1 F6

### Le Central Restaurant
**La Cigale Hotel, Fereej Bin Mahmoud**

Mediterranean
4428 8888

Surrounded on three sides by floor-to-ceiling glass, Le Central offers great views and is so bright you may need sunglasses. You can order off the a la carte menu, or opt for the three-course business lunch, which changes every week. You can also pay QR 90 to eat from the salad bar, which isn't piled high like some buffets. **Map** 1 F5

### Le Cigalon Restaurant
**La Cigale Hotel, Fereej Bin Mahmoud**

International
4428 8888

This bright and modern buffet restaurant features a giant aquarium alongside amber and grey leather seats. There are plenty of salads and a few hot choices – the emphasis is on Lebanese food with unusual dishes like kibbeh shishbarak (couscous and meat patties cooked in yoghurt). La Cigale flies most of its fresh food in from Lebanon every day. It isn't cheap, but the quality and food is impressive – the cheese counter alone stocks 180 different kinds. **Map** 1 F5

### Lobby Lounge
**InterContinental Doha The City, Onaiza**

Cafes & Coffee Shops
4015 8888

Head here for one of Doha's finest afternoon tea sessions. What ever you pick from the tray, the use of high quality, seasonal ingredients is evident and, in addition to classic smoked salmon sandwiches and other traditional items, specialities such as Ajwa date scones add a regional touch. Enjoy it all with a glass of bubbly or a pot of delicate Jing tea; organic, fair-trade green tea is also available. **Map** 1 G1

### The Lobby Lounge
Cafes & Coffee Shops
The Ritz-Carlton, Doha, Al Gassar
4484 8000

The Ritz-Carlton is not known for its afternoon tea for nothing. Relax to live music performances on the harp and piano in the luxurious comfort of grandiose furnishings, all the while sampling a classic and exquisite afternoon tea presented with guaranteed Ritz-Carlton finesse. **Map** 3 D1

### Market by Jean-Georges
International
W Doha Hotel & Residences, Al Dafna
4453 5000

This trendy haunt has wowed its guests thanks to unusual flavour and texture combos. The black truffle and fontina pizza is among the perennial favourites and whether you turn up for a business lunch or an evening with friends, the innovative twists on comfort foods will add a wow-factor. You'll also find perfectly traditional items such as rotisserie chicken with mashed potatoes, while the health-conscious can choose between grilled fish and salads. The Friday Jazz Brunch is popular. **Map** 1 H1

### Mawasem
International
Hilton Doha
4423 3333

The food here covers every continent, with well-known dishes from Europe through to Asia. Choose from grilled meats, seafood platters, sushi and tasty Indian curries. If the restaurant's live-cooking station doesn't keep you inside, there is also a pleasant terrace for outdoor dining. As well as the la carte options, buffets are available for breakfast, lunch and dinner, so there is plenty of choice. **Map** 1 J1

## Megu
Japanese

Porto Arabia, The Pearl  
4495 3876

It's abundantly clear that Megu is set to be special as you ride in a private lift to the restaurant's main entrance. Entering the plush surroundings is a visually stunning experience thanks to beautiful alcoves and high ceilings. Megu serves Japanese cuisine with a modern twist that turns sushi dishes into creative masterpieces. The kobe beef will have you salivating for days. **Map** 3 D2

## Neo Restaurant
International

Souq Najad, Salwa Rd, New Al Mirqab  
4432 2508

Although it serves an international mix, Neo is best known for its sushi and fans of this Japanese treat shouldn't miss the weekly Tuesday night sushi feast. You pay a set fee and it just keeps coming; fresh, tender and undoubtedly the best in Doha. With dark wood, channels of pebbles and subdued lighting, the restaurant has a Japanese feel. Neo prides itself on preparing everything from scratch, from bread to ice cream, and you'll taste the difference. **Map** 1 F6

## The Old Manor
Steakhouse

Mercure Grand Hotel Doha City Centre, Al Jasra  
4446 2222

A cross between a gentlemen's club and an English public house, The Old Manor offers firm favourites including shepherd's pie, chicken in a basket and steaks. The cosy little venue is casual and relaxed, with a big-screen TV and comfy chairs. With a great view over the city centre, this is the perfect place to tuck into a pie and a pint. **Map** 1 G5

## Going Out — Restaurants & Cafes

### Opal By Gordon Ramsay
**International**
St Regis Doha, Al Gassar
4446 0000

This chic bistro manages to strike the fine balance between upscale and relaxed. The dining area is open and lively, while the menu features contemporary international cuisine. Some unusual combinations help turn the dining experience into a culinary adventure. The gourmet pizzas and molecular cocktails are worth a try. Despite offering some fine food in a fun, classy setting, the restaurant's prices remain a notch below most high-end establishments  **Map** 3 D2

### Orangery Cafe Trottoir
**Cafes & Coffee Shops**
La Cigale, Fereej Bin Mahmoud
4428 8888

With enormous windows and a lovely terrace, this cafe boasts a wonderfully bright and airy feel: in short, it's the perfect venue for a light lunch. The menu ranges from shawarmas to pizza, crepes and waffles, and wonderfully fresh juices and mocktails are available to wash it all down.  **Map** 1 F5

### Paloma
**Tex Mex**
InterContinental Doha, Al Gassar
4484 4444

A spicy Latino atmosphere awaits everyone at this lively Mexican restaurant where good food, entertainment and a superb choice of beverages are found in abundance. The interior is dominated by the large dancefloor, which gives Paloma a suitable feel to double up as a nightlife haunt, so it's a bit different for Doha. If the generally good band is a bit much for your tastes, a quieter evening can be enjoyed on the outside terrace overlooking the pool.  **Map** 3 D2

*Opal By Gordon Ramsay*

Going Out

Restaurants & Cafes

### Ponderosa
American  
Nr Ramada Junction, Salwa Rd, New Al Mirqab    4465 5880  
This firmly established restaurant chain offers an enjoyable and energetic dining experience that's particularly suited for families with young children. The menu concentrates on tried and tested staples from steak and chicken to seafood, or you could opt for the popular all-you-can-eat buffet. **Map** 1 F6

### Porcini
Italian  
The Ritz-Carlton Doha, Al Gassar    4484 8000  
Widely accepted as the best Italian restaurant in Qatar, Porcini delivers an exceptional dining experience. The luxurious, opulent and stylish furnishings radiate the charm and comfort of a cosy lounge room, the delectable menu offers culinary treats from across Italy, while the extensive wine selection is sure to impress even the pickiest connoisseur. Added to this, service is impeccable and should you wish to try something different, private cooking classes are also available. **Map** 3 D1

### Prime
Steakhouse  
InterContinental Doha The City, West Bay    4015 8888  
Prime has boosted Doha's dining scene and is a treat for meat-lovers in the city. This eatery is a bold, quality meat restaurant that offers the finest selection of cuts in a comfortable and elegant setting. Prime promotes flexible dining, where guests can choose a live-grilling station, an interactive dining experience or retreat into a cosy private dining area. **Map** 1 G2

### Richoux
**City Center Doha, Al Dafna**

International
4493 1661

A surprising yet welcome touch of class among City Center Doha's many eateries, Richoux's dark woodwork, red leather seats and gold-coloured railings and light fittings are a world away from the shops just outside. One side of the menu features breakfast, pastries and a full traditional afternoon tea for two. Flip the menu over and you'll find a choice of sandwiches, starters and mains. **Map** 1 H1

### Salsa
**Doha Marriott Hotel, Al Khulaifat**

Mexican
4429 8464

Serving classic Latin favourites from sizzling fajitas to big steaks and a choice of enchiladas, this lively Mexican restaurant is a great place to come with friends. There are also lighter options of tasty salads on the menu, but portions are generous and most mains are served with refried beans and Mexican rice. The live band will put everybody in a party mood – and help you dance off your dinner. **Map** 1 K4

> **Afternoon Tea**
>
> Several of the top hotels in the city offer high tea; some of the standouts include Al Jalsa at Sharq Village Hotel & Spa (4425 6666), The Lobby Lounge at the Ritz-Carlton (4484 8000) and Seasons Tea Lounge at the Four Seasons (4494 8888). Each venue handles the tradition flawlessly – a Doha must.

### Seasons Restaurant

Mediterranean

Mövenpick Hotel Doha, Slata 4429 1111

This restaurant has a variety of theme nights including French, Swiss, Asian and seafood. The Friday brunch is also popular, where kids are not only welcomed, but also supervised and well-entertained. The all-you-can-eat buffet may not be as large as some of the other hotels, but the seafood and sushi are outstanding and the cheese is excellent. **Map** 1 J4

### Shawarma Albisana

Arabic

Katara Cultural Village, Al Gassar 4408 1400

Arabian style fastfood is on offer at this family friendly restaurant. The setting reminds you of a French-style bistro, but the food is Lebanese and choosing is superbly easy as there are just two main options: chicken or beef shawarma served with optional sides of chopped parsley, onions, potatoes and chilli paste. On a Tuesday you can splash out on a rather unique combination: Japanese Wagyu beef shawarma. **Map** 3 D2

### Shisha Garden

Arabic

La Cigale Hotel, Fereej Bin Mahmoud 4428 8888

This is one of the best spots in town for a casual and relaxed evening over some authentic hubbly bubbly. Best enjoyed in the evening, the creatively designed garden cafe is a great spot for a meet-up with family and friends. Sports fans will be treated to huge screens in almost every corner of the terrace. When hunger strikes, opt for a selection of mezze. **Map** 1 F5

Going Out

### Spice Market
**W Doha Hotel & Residences, Al Dafna**

South-East Asian
4453 5000

Spice Market mixes moody red lighting and Arabic lanterns with Oriental-inspired black ash furniture. Fans of Asian cuisine will be spoilt for choice, but the good news is that everything comes in 'family style' sharing portions. The highlights include blackened shrimps with sun-dried pineapple, lobster cake and mango salad. To top it off, there's a selection of innovative cocktails. **Map** 1 H1

### The Square
**InterContinental Doha The City, Onaiza**

International
4015 8888

Whether you go a la carte or turn up for the buffet option, the choice is broad. The brunch (QR 290 per person including bubbly) offers a tasty selection of international cuisines hailing from Thailand, India, Italy and Japan – to name but a few. In the evening, only half of the cooking stations are open, but the food is no less impressive. Choose between meat and seafood mains, or opt for pizzas and pasta. **Map** 1 G1

### Strata
**InterContinental Doha The City, Onaiza**

Seafood
4015 8888

Located on the 55th floor, this is high-end dining on more levels than one. The set menu offers a five course culinary journey, or you could go a la carte to sample whatever fine delicacy strikes your fancy. The food is accompanied with some irresistible bread, and an excellent selection of wine to complete the picture when the occasion calls for something special. **Map** 1 G1

### Sukhar Pasha Ottoman Lounge  Turkish
Katara Cultural Village, Al Gassar  4408 2000

At first glance, this relaxing haunt may appear to be a shisha lounge. However, while the hubbly bubbly (the traditional Arabic water pipe through which fruity tobacco is smoked) is certainly top-notch, it's the food that ends up stealing the show. Authentic and delicious, even the simple vegetable casserole is good enough to leave you begging for the recipe. The hot and cold mezze is particularly highly-regarded among those in the know. **Map** 3 D2

### Taj Rasoi  Indian
Doha Marriott Hotel, Al Khulaifat  4429 8470

Serving specialities from around India, Taj Rasoi offers diners traditional dishes cooked with great skill. The mouthwatering menu of various tandoori dishes, curries and breads will leave you both impressed and with a full stomach. Many dishes are also prepared at the table so you'll gain an insight into the secrets of Indian cooking. **Map** 1 K4

### Tajine  Moroccan
Souk Waqif, Al Jasra  4435 5554

Dim light shines out of brass lamps and reflects off ornately carved wood trim, making Tajine a perfect spot for a romantic night out or quiet evening with friends. The menu revolves around the traditional tajine – a covered clay pot used for both cooking and serving. Moroccan food tends to rely on spices, and the resulting flavour is earthy and mellow. **Map** 1 H4

### Tangia
Moroccan
Wyndham Grand Regency Doha, Al Sadd — 4434 3333

With only a few local restaurants serving Moroccan food, Tangia attracts diners in search of a spicy tagine or hearty couscous. The dishes dispatched by the skilled chef contain unique flavours and aromas and all are artistically prepared and extravagantly served. The scent of coriander, cumin and saffron adds to the experience. **Map** 1 E4

### The Fork & Knife
International
Mövenpick Tower & Suites Doha, Al Dafna — 4496 6666

This new restaurant has a great atmosphere, a modern interior and is family-friendly. The skilled chefs serve up an international buffet every day for breakfast, lunch and dinner. Choose from a wide selection of tasty Arabic, Indian and European dishes and desserts. This hotel is 'dry' but the mocktails are faultless, and the ginger and lemongrass water is delicious. **Map** 1 H1

### The Tent
Arabic
Al Bustan Hotel, Slata — 4432 8888

As soon as you enter The Tent, the traditional design of the furniture, the soft lighting and the aroma of shisha will awaken your senses to this truly Middle Eastern experience. The food is a fantastic example of Arabic cooking and the waiters are more than happy to help make ordering easier by recommending a few of their favourite dishes. It's a good spot for a romantic evening or to relax after a long day, but reservations are recommended. **Map** 1 J4

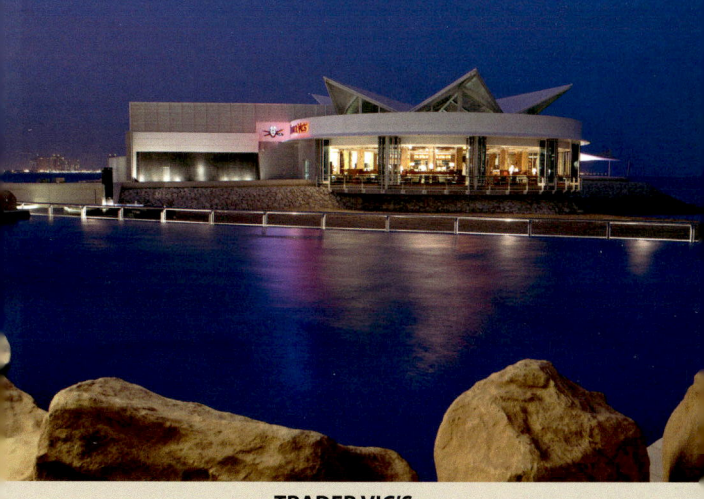

## TRADER VIC'S
## AT HILTON DOHA

Lunch: 12pm-3pm
Dinner: 7pm-11:30pm
Friday Brunch: 12:30pm-3pm
Happy Hour: Daily from 5pm-8pm

Dress Code: Smart Casual, Local dress welcome

For bookings please call 4423 3117

**TRADER VIC'S**

### Thai Noodles
Nr Souq Aseiry, Al Mahmal St, Al Souq

Far Eastern
4443 4220

Tucked away in the heart of the souk area, you might need help finding this little piece of Thailand in Doha – but it's worth the effort. As you enter, you are greeted with big smiles and the aromas of traditional Thai cooking. Open for breakfast, lunch and dinner, the extensive menu offers a huge choice of Thai and oriental dishes. The popularity of this place speaks volumes about the excellent food. **Map** 1 H4

### Trader Vic's
Hilton Doha

Asian-Polynesian
4423 3333

Trader Vic's is a popular restaurant serves an eclectic selection of Asian-Polynesian dishes and signature dishes from an innovative a la carte menu. Famous for their tropical drinks list, settle in on the terrace for sunset and a selection of exotic beverages and don't leave without trying their trademark Mai Tai. Relax and enjoy vibrant music from their live Cuban band. **Map** 1 J1

### Trattoria
Concorde Hotel, Doha

Italian
4407 3333

If you are dining out for a special occasion and in the mood for an Italian, then look no further than Trattoria. The airy and light setting with its wooden floors and cream and brown colour scheme makes this a smart-casual affair. The appetising menu offers a delicious selection of pizzas, fresh salads and the tempting pasta dishes will lure you back for more. **Map** 2 E6

### Tse Yang
Chinese
Porto Arabia, The Pearl  4495 3876

The menu includes everything from dim sum to Peking duck, all of which are masterfully created the restaurant's Chinese chef. It's a good idea to step out of your comfort zone and ask for recommendations. If in doubt, the honey roasted chicken, deep fried squid and Peking duck are among the favourites here. And portions are on the generous side, so bring your appetite. **Map** 3 D2

### Victoria
International
Grand Heritage Doha Hotel & Spa, Baaya  4445 5555

This tea lounge resembles a classic Victorian library with dark wood panelling and antique English and Arabic books lining one wall. The atmosphere is quiet and refined, perfect for a traditional afternoon tea. Individual tea pots are presented beautifully and the accompanying stand of treats – ranging from mini quiches and sandwiches to dainty pastries – is substantial enough for two people to share. **Map** 3 A5

### Yen Sushi Bar
Japanese
La Cigale Hotel, Fereej Bin Mahmoud  4428 8888

Located in La Cigale's lobby, this intimate sushi bar can only accommodate 18 people around its rotating belt. Diners can peer over the moving sashimi and watch the masterful chefs prepare some of the best sushi in town. A few tables line the perimeter of the bar, but be sure to sit up close if you want to enjoy the full experience. **Map** 1 F5

## Nightlife Establishments

**Doha's nightlife scene has improved in recent years and there's now a decent selection of clubs, lounges and other venues to choose from.**

### Admiral's Club
**The Ritz-Carlton Doha, Al Gassar**    4484 8000

Set away from the hotel in a separate building by the marina, this popular club seems to pick up around 11pm and goes on until 3am. During the cooler months, it has a wonderful outdoor space overlooking the yachts moored below.
**Map** 3 D1

### Cigar Lounge
**Sharq Village & Spa, Al Khulaifat**    4425 6666

Appropriately dark and stately, this classic cigar lounge appeals to both the aficionado and the occasional smoker. Choose from an impressive collection of cigars or select one of the in-house options, which are rolled on the spot. Don't miss the uniquely designed ceiling fans that sway gently back and forth. **Map** 1 K5

### Crystal
**W Doha Hotel & Residences**    4453 5000

A welcome addition to Doha's nightlife scene, this dark and funky venue features black chandeliers and bold prints in moody colours. Crystal gets crammed at the weekend, with Doha's bold and beautiful mingling to the DJs soundtrack. It's a place to be seen, so dress to impress. **Map** 1 H1

## Habanos

The Ritz-Carlton Doha, Al Gassar    4484 8000

With rich reds and dark mahogany, Habanos has an intimate and cosy feel, and in the cooler weather you can relax outside on the attractive terrace. The cocktails are divine, and little touches like the complimentary snacks add to the experience.
**Map** 3 D1

## Hive

InterContinental Doha The City, Onaiza    4015 8888

The Hive's chic, relaxed atmosphere makes it a popular choice for after work beverages. Two televisions screen sports channels so footie fans can also catch a match over a glass or two. On Wednesdays, you get to take advantage of the weekly wine and cheese night (QR 180).  **Map** 1 G1

**Going Out**

### Jazz At The Lincoln
St Regis Doha, Al Gassar       4446 0300

For a night of nostalgia and top-notch live music, this is a delightful way to start any weekend. With views out to sea and the sultry sounds of Sinatra, enjoy a delicious savoury snack or try their amazing chocolate and salted caramel tart. An elegant venue to really appreciate jazz. **Map** 3 D2

### Jazz Up Bar
Mövenpick Hotel Doha, Slata       4429 1111

Fans of jazz and chilled out vibes will be right at home at this intimate venue. The cocktail menu features some interesting concoctions and, if you get a little peckish, a good selection of light bites is also, on offer. **Map** 1 J4

### Zero Tolerance
Qatar has a zero tolerance rule when it comes to driving under the influence of alcohol. Anyone caught faces huge fines and even jail time. There are plenty of taxis stationed outside the main hotels, and it's never usually a problem to hail one down.

### Lava
InterContinental Doha
4484 4444

Lava has really managed to heat up Doha's party scene, and it always pulls a good crowd. Fiery orange lighting sets the scene and whether a live band or a DJ is in charge of the sounds, it won't take long for the place to fill up. The outdoors terrace grants great skyline views of Doha. **Map** 3 E2

### The Library Bar & Cigar Lounge
Four Seasons Hotel, Al Dafna    4494 8888

Surrounded by leather buttoned chairs, you can't help but relax at the Library Bar. Abstract art hanging from the dark wood walls adds to the ambience of the gentlemen's club setting. Take your pick from the cigar and food menu while enjoying the splendid sea views, or the music from the pianist who plays every night from 8pm. **Map** 1 H1

### The Lounge
Kempinski Residences & Suites, Doha, Al Dafna    4405 3325

This upscale venue's dark walls, minimalist decor and dim lighting create a sophisticated setting for beverages and light bites. Smooth cocktails, savoury nibbles and delectable desserts grace the menu, while the resident pianist's renditions of George Gershwin and Irving Berlin add to the elegantly moody vibe. If you're feeling peckish, the tasting menu is perfect for groups of two or more looking to share some late-night nosh with finesse. **Map** 1 H1

### Pearl Lounge Club
Doha Marriott Hotel, Al Khulaifat    4429 8444

This smart club has a reputation for being rather exclusive – and for mixing perfect cocktails. Completely separate from the hotel, it has its own identity, playing ambient music early evening then switching to a variety of more upbeat styles later on. Only members and guests can come on weekend nights, but on other nights, if you look smart, you should be welcome. **Map** 1 K4

askexplorer.com

## Qube

**Radisson Blu Hotel, Doha, Rawdat Al Khail**     4428 1555

This cavernous nightclub buried deep in the Radisson Blu complex is one of the newer clubs in Doha and is most definitely one of the largest. It offers a mixture of live music, visiting DJs and has special nights for hip-hop, UK dance and Indian music. It's got a VIP area and Doha's longest counter. The entry fee of QR 80 might be a bit steep, but it includes your first beverage; ladies get in free. **Map** 1 F6

## Seven

**La Cigale Hotel, Fereej Bin Mahmoud**     4428 8888

With an all-white decor, smoke machines and thumping beats, this club boasts an unashamedly showy Euro-pop vibe. The resident DJ's house tunes keep the revellers going on the club's sunken dancefloor, as do the tasty (if somewhat pricey) cocktails; free soda is served to those who opt for whole bottles. The price of an annual membership card (QR 100) is offset against the QR 200. **Map** 1 F5

## Wahm

**W Doha Hotel & Residences**     4453 5000

Set out by the W Hotel's pool, Wahm is more than a standard pool haunt: the modern majlis seating and a generally laidback vibe set the scene, and the contemporary Arabic theme continues on through to the mezze snacks on offer and to the vibrantly coloured oriental decor that kits out the venue. Settle down to some shisha in an al fresco cabana and you'll never want to leave. **Map** 1 H1

Going Out

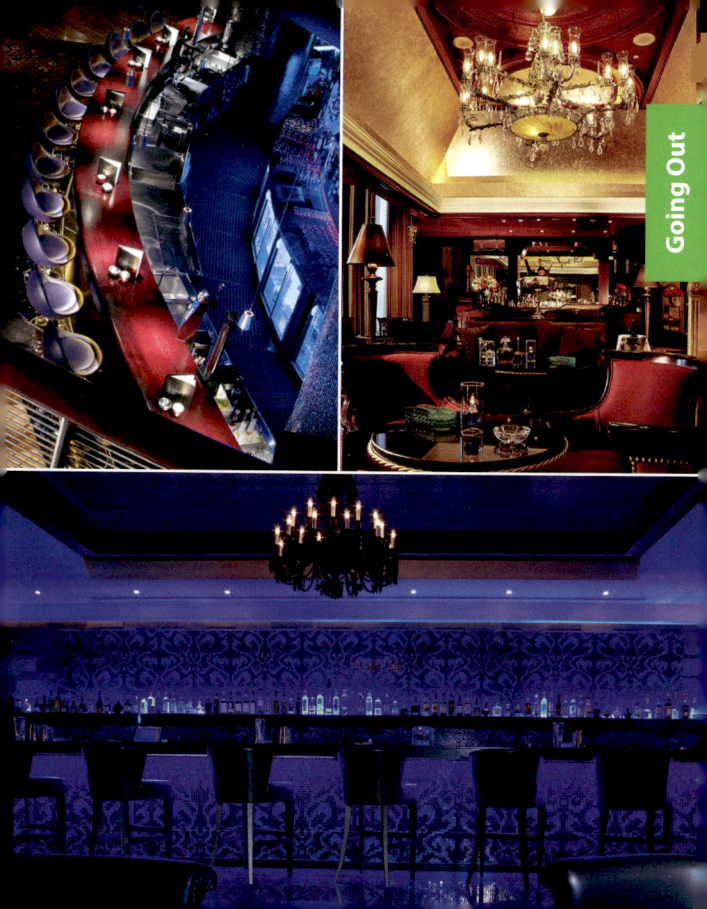

# Index

## A

| | |
|---|---|
| AAB Rent-A-Car Company | 53 |
| Accommodation | 56 |
| Active Qatar | 116 |
| Admiral's Club | 220 |
| Air Arabia | 33 |
| Air India | 33 |
| Airlines | 33 |
| Al Aziziya | 92, 184 |
| Al Bidda Park | 84 |
| Al Bustan Hotel | 66 |
| Al Dafna | 76, 180 |
| Al Dafna, Al Gassar & West Bay | 181 |
| Al Dana | 186 |
| Al Gassar | 184 |
| Al Hamra | 186 |
| Al Hasbah | 187 |
| Al Jassasiyeh Carvings | 104 |
| Al Khaima | 187 |
| Al Khor Fly-In | 47 |
| Al Khor Museum | 105 |
| Al Koot Fort Museum | 98 |
| Al Liwan | 187 |
| Al Luqta Street | 88, 183 |
| Al Majlis | 188 |
| Al Markhiya Gallery | 100 |
| Al Mirqab Street | 146 |
| Al Mourjan | 188 |
| Al Muftah Rent A Car | 53 |
| Al Muntazah Park | 92 |
| Al Rakiyat Fort | 105 |
| Al Rayyan Road | 72, 182 |
| Al Sadd Road | 72, 182 |
| Al Sadd Street | 146 |
| Al Sayyad | 188 |
| Al Shaqab Stud | 88 |
| Al Sulaiman Rent A Car | 53 |
| Al Wajbah Fort | 72 |
| Albatross Restaurant | 190 |
| Albisana Kunafa | 190 |
| Alcohol | 13, 37 |
| Alison Nelson's Chocolate Bar | 190 |
| Almana Rent A Car – Hertz | 53 |
| American Grill | 191 |
| Angsana Spa | 138 |
| Animal Souk | 92 |
| Annual Events | 46 |
| Apollo Furniture | 146 |
| Arabian Adventures | 112 |
| Arabic | 38, 176 |
| Architecture | 70 |
| Area Directory | 180 |
| Aroma | 191 |
| Art | 70 |
| Ascott Doha | 66 |
| ...ADVERT | 67 |
| Asia Live! | 191 |
| Aspire Academy For Sports Excellence | 120, 134 |
| Aspire Park | 134 |
| Aspire Zone | 120, 134 |
| ...ADVERT | vi |
| Assaha Lebanese Traditional Village | 192 |
| Astor Grill At St Regis | 192 |
| Automatic | 192 |
| Avis | 53 |

## B

| | |
|---|---|
| Bahrain Air | 33 |
| Bargaining | 148 |
| Bay Club | 119 |
| Beijing | 193 |

Qatar **Visitors'** Guide

# Index

| | |
|---|---|
| Beirut Restaurant | 193 |
| Bicycles | 50 |
| Bistro 61 | 193 |
| Black Pearl | 113 |
| Bliss Spa | 138 |
| Blogs | 43 |
| Blue | 194 |
| Blue Salon | 160 |
| Boat Tours | 110 |
| Boats | 51 |
| Books & Maps | 43 |
| Budget Rent A Car | 53 |
| Burj Al Hamam | 194 |
| Bus | 51 |

## C

| | |
|---|---|
| Cafe Amici | 194 |
| Cafe Bateel | 196 |
| Cafes | 176, 186 |
| Calls To Prayer | 14 |
| Camel Racing | 132 |
| Camel Racing Track | 112 |
| Camel Rides | 118 |
| Camping | 30, 66, 118 |
| Car Hire | 52 |
| Carpets | 162 |
| Cathay Pacific Airways | 33 |
| Central Market | 147 |
| Centrepoint | 154 |
| Century Hotel | 66 |
| Chopsticks | 196 |
| Ciao | 196 |
| Cigar Lounge | 220 |
| Cinema | 172 |
| City Center Doha | 154 |
| ...ADVERT | IBC, 155 |
| City Tours | 111 |
| Climate | 36 |
| Comedy | 172 |
| Commercial Bank of Qatar | |
| ...ADVERT | IFC |
| Commercial Bank | |
| Qatar Masters | 46 |
| Commercialbank Grand | |
| Prix Of Qatar | 48 |
| Concerts | 173 |
| Concorde Hotel | 58 |
| ...ADVERT | 59 |
| Corniche | 197 |
| Cosmo | 197 |
| Country Tours | 112 |
| Courtyard By Marriott | 58 |
| Crepaway | 197 |
| Crime | 36 |
| Crystal | 220 |
| Cuisine | 170 |
| Cultural Village of Katara | 78 |
| Customs | 33 |
| Cycling | 84, 132 |

## D

| | |
|---|---|
| Dahal Al Hamam Park | 88 |
| Delta Airlines | 33 |
| Department Stores | 160 |
| Desert Safaris | 116 |
| Dhow Charters | 119 |
| Dhow Dinner Cruises | 25 |
| Di Capri | 198 |
| Dine At The Pearl | 23 |
| Diplomatic Club, The | 125, 129 |
| Diving | 120 |
| Doha Corniche | 82, 183 |
| Doha Fort | 98 |
| Doha Golf Club | 121 |
| Doha International Airport | 32 |
| Doha Jazz Festival | 46 |
| Doha Marriott Hotel | 60 |
| Doha Sub Aqua Club (DSAC) | 120 |
| Doha Film Festival | 48 |
| Door Policy | 169 |
| Dos & Don'ts | 36 |
| Drinking | 170 |
| Driving | 52 |
| Drugs | 37 |
| Dune Bashing | 26, 127 |

## E

| | |
|---|---|
| Eating Out | 169 |
| Economy | 16 |
| Education City | 89 |
| Egypt Air | 33 |
| Eid Al Adha | 44, 49 |
| Eid Al Fitr | 44, 48 |
| Electricity | 37 |
| Emirates Airline | 33 |
| Entertainment | 172 |
| Equestrian Sports | 133 |
| Etihad Airways | 33 |
| Euro Dollar Rent A Car | 53 |
| Europcar | 53 |

## F

| | |
|---|---|
| Fashion Shows | 174 |
| Fasting | 14 |
| Fauchon | 198 |
| Female Visitors | 37 |
| Fereej Bin Mahmoud | 183 |
| FIFA | 134 |
| FIFA World Cup | 5, 116 |
| Fish Market | 94 |
| Fishing | 121 |

askexplorer.com

227

# Index

| | | | | | |
|---|---|---|---|---|---|
| Flavours | 199 | InterContinental Doha | 61 | Lagoon, The | 204 |
| Football | 133 | InterContinental Doha | | Lagoona Mall | 155 |
| Friday Market | 149 | The City | 61 | Landmark Shopping Mall | 155 |
| Fuddruckers | 199 | Internet | 41 | Language | 38 |
| Fun City | 73 | Islam | 14 | Laughter Factory, The | 172 |
| | | Islamic Art | 24 | Lava | 222 |

## G

Garden Restaurant, The 200
Giant 155
Gold Souk 150
Golf 121, 134
Gondolania 94
Gourmet House 200
Grand Heritage Hotel 58
Grand Hyatt 60
Grand Mosque 111
Gulf Adventures Tourism 113, 127
Gulf Air 33

## H

Habanos 221
Hamad Int'l Airport 18, 32, 40
Hakkasan 199
Haram 13
Highland 160
Hilton Doha 60
...*ADVERT* 57
Hive 221
Horse Riding 122
Horses 91
Hotel Apartments 70
Hwang 200
Hyatt Plaza 155

## I

I-Net Cafe 76
Il Teatro 202

## J

J&G Sandwich Cellar 202
Japanese 178
Jarir Bookstore 146
Jaula Spa 139
Jazz At The Lincoln 222
Jazz Up Bar 222
Jewellery & Watches 162
Johnny Rockets 202
Jungle Zone 95
JW's Steakhouse 203

## K

K108 Hotel 61
Katara Cultural Village 78, 124
Katara International
Kites Family Day 48
Katara Village 27
Kayaking 122
Kempinski Residences
& Suites Doha 62
Khalifa Street 88, 183
Khor Al Adaid 108
Kitesurfing 124

## L

L'Wzaar Seafood Restaurant 203
La Cigale Hotel 62
La Mer 203
La Villa 204

Layali Restaurant 204
Le Central Restaurant 205
Le Cigalon Restaurant 205
Le Park Hotel 66
Lexus Tailors 164
Library Bar & Cigar
Lounge, The 223
Live Music 173
Lobby Lounge 205
Lounge, The 223
Lufthansa 33

## M

Magazines 42
Mall, The 156
Mannai Autorent 53
Maps 43
Market By Jean-Georges 206
Markets & Souks 148
Marks & Spencer 161
Mathaf Arab Museum
Of Modern Art 89
Mawasem 206
Mediterranean 178
Megu 207
Merch 161
Mercure Grand Hotel
Doha City Centre 66
Mexican 178
MICE Market 4, 18
Moroccan 178

| | | |
|---|---|---|
| Motorsports | 130, 135 | |
| Mövenpick Hotel Doha | 66 | |
| Museum Of Islamic Art | 82 | |
| Museum Park | 84 | |
| Musheirib | 146 | |
| Mustafawi Limousine | 53 | |

## N

| | |
|---|---|
| National Car Rental | 53 |
| National Day | 49 |
| Neo Restaurant | 207 |
| Newspapers & Magazines | 42 |

## O

| | |
|---|---|
| Oil | 9 |
| Old Manor, The | 207 |
| Omani Market | 149 |
| Onaiza | 183 |
| Ooredoo | 41 |
| Opal By Gordon Ramsay | 208 |
| Orangery Cafe Trottoir | 208 |
| Orientalist Museum | 100 |
| Oryx Farm | 108 |
| Oryx Rotana | 62 |
| Ottoman Empire | 8 |

## P

| | |
|---|---|
| Palm Tree Island Boat Company | 119 |
| Paloma | 208 |
| Parasailing | 124 |
| Park | 29 |
| Pearl Divers | 120 |
| Pearl Lounge Club | 223 |
| Pearl, The | 78, 156, 185 |
| Persian Carpets | 162 |
| Places Of Worship | 111 |

| | |
|---|---|
| Places To Stay | 56 |
| Police | 40 |
| Ponderosa | 210 |
| Porcini | 210 |
| Pork | 13 |
| Powerboat Racing | 47, 136 |
| Powerboating | 125 |
| Prestige Rent A Car | 53 |
| Prime | 210 |
| Public Holidays | 44 |

## Q

| | |
|---|---|
| Q-Dive Marine Center | 120, 127 |
| Qatar Airways | 33 |
| Qatar Checklist | 20 |
| Qatar ExxonMobil Open Tennis Tournament | 46 |
| Qatar International Adventures | 113 |
| Qatar International Equestrian Festival | 47 |
| Qatar International Rally | 135 |
| Qatar International Regatta | 47 |
| Qatar International Tours | 118, 121, 126, 128 |
| Qatar Kitesurfing Club | 124 |
| Qatar Ladies Open | 47 |
| Qatar Motor & Motorcycle Federation | 136 |
| Qatar National Heritage Library | 95 |
| Qatar National Museum | 84 |
| Qatar Racing & Equestrian Club | 122, 133 |
| Qatar Sailing & Rowing Federation | 125 |

| | |
|---|---|
| Qatari Diar Real Estate Investment | |
| ...*ADVERT* | ii-iii |
| Quad Bikes | 125 |
| Qube | 224 |

## R

| | |
|---|---|
| Radio | 43 |
| Radisson Blu | 66 |
| Ray's Reef | 73 |
| Regatta Sailing Academy | 111, 126 |
| Remede | 143 |
| Restaurants | 176, 186 |
| Richoux | 211 |
| Ritz-Carlton Doha, The | 63 |
| Ronautica Middle East | 121, 128 |
| Royal Jordanian | 33 |
| Royal Plaza | 158 |
| Rumeilah Park (Al Bidda Park) | 84 |

## S

| | |
|---|---|
| Safari Tours | 112 |
| Safety | 36 |
| Safir Doha Hotel | 66 |
| Sailing | 125 |
| Salam Plaza | 161 |
| Salsa | 211 |
| Salwa Road | 92, 146, 184 |
| Sand Boarding | 126 |
| Saudi Arabian Airlines | 33 |
| Sealine Beach Resort | 118, 122, 125 |
| Seasons Restaurant | 212 |
| Seven | 224 |
| Sharq Village & Spa | 56, 63 |
| Shawarma Albisana | 212 |
| Sheikh Faisal Museum | 112 |

# Index

Sheraton Doha Resort & Convention Hotel — 63
Shisha Cafes — 171
Shisha Garden — 212
Shopping — 144
Shopping Malls — 154
Sightseeing — 110
Singapore Airlines — 33
Six Senses Spa — 140
Skate Shack — 146
Slata — 184
Snorkelling — 127
Somerset West Bay — 64
Souk Al Ahmed — 152
Souk Al Asiery — 152
Souk Al Dira — 152
Souk Al Jabor — 152
Souk Area — 98, 184
Souk Haraj — 153
Souk Nasser Bin Saif — 153
Souk Waqif — 150, 184
Souks — 148
Souvenirs — 163
Spa & Wellness Centre — 140
Spa, The Ritz-Carlton Doha — 139
Spas — 138
Spectator Sports — 130
Spice Market — 214
Square, The — 214
Squash — 136
St Regis Doha — 64
...ADVERT — 65
Steakhouse — 179
Strata — 214
Sukhar Pasha
  Ottoman Lounge — 215
Swiss-Belhotel Doha — 66

## T

Tailoring & Textiles — 164
Taj Rasoi — 215
Tajine — 215
Tangia — 216
Taxis — 32, 53
Telephone — 41
Television — 42
Tennis — 137
Tent, The — 216
Textiles — 164
Thai Noodles — 218
The Cultural — 27
The Diplomatic Club — 125, 129
The Fish Market — 198
The Fork & Knife — 216
The Garden Restaurant — 200
The Lobby Lounge — 206
The Mall — 156
The Pearl — 78, 156, 185
Theatre — 174
Thrifty Car Rental — 53
Thursday & Friday Market — 149
Time — 41
Tipping — 41
Tour Operators — 112
Tours — 110
Trader Vic's — 218
...ADVERT — 217
Trattoria — 218
Tse Yang — 219
Turkish Airlines — 33

## U

Umm Salal Mohammed Fort — 108

## V

Venue Directory — 176
Victoria — 219
Villaggio Mall — 158
Visas — 33
Visitor Information — 34

## W

Wadi Bashing — 127
Wahm — 224
Wakeboarding — 128
Walking — 54
Watches — 162
Water — 37
Websites & Blogs — 43
West Bay — 76, 180
Windtower House — 100

## Y

Yen Sushi Bar — 219

## Z

ZigZag Towers — 144
Zubarah — 106
Zubarah Boutique Hotel — 64
Zubarah Fort — 106

Notes

# Notes

Notes

# explorer

**Explorer Products**

Check out ask**explorer**.com/shop

### Residents' Guides

Abu Dhabi | Azerbaijan | Dubai | Oman | Qatar

### Visitors' Guides

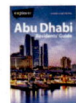

Abu Dhabi | Baku | Bahrain | Dubai | Qatar | Sharjah

### Photography Books & Calendars

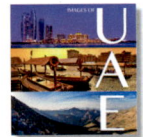

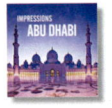

234  Qatar **Visitors'** Guide

## Maps

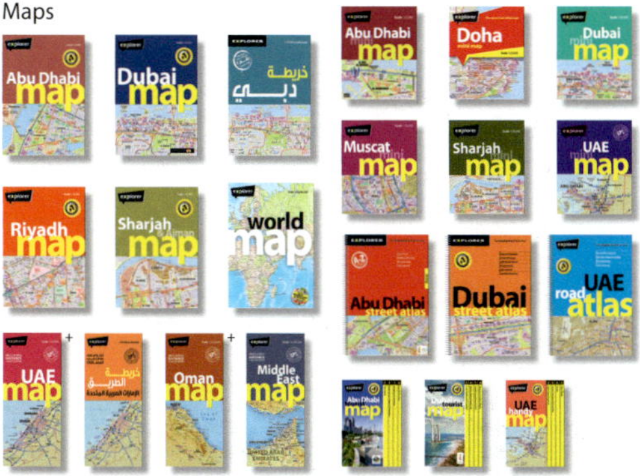

## Adventure & Lifestyle Guides

## Apps & eBooks

+ Also available as applications.
Visit askexplorer.com/apps.

* Now available in eBook format.

**Visit askexplorer.com/shop for a full product list.**

askexplorer.com

# Explorer Team

Check out ask**explorer**.com

### Publishing
**Chief Content Officer & Founder**
Alistair MacKenzie

### Editorial
**Managing Editor** Carli Allan
**Editors** Lily Lawes, Kirsty Tuxford, Lisa Crowther
**Research Manager** Mimi Stankova
**Researchers** Amrit Raj, Roja P, Praseena, Shalu Sukumar, Maria Luisa Reyes, Lara Santizo, Jayleen Aguinaldo, Jacqueline Reyes, Yuliya Molchanova

### Design & Photography
**Art Director** Ieyad Charaf
**Layout Manager** Jayde Fernandes
**Junior Designer** M. Shakkeer
**Cartography Manager** Zain Madathil
**Cartographers** Noushad Madathil, Dhanya Nellikkunnummal, Ramla Kambravan, Jithesh Kalathingal
**GIS Analyst** Aslam Jobydas KD
**Photographer & Image Editor** Hardy Mendrofa

### Sales
**Director of Sales** Peter Saxby
**Media Sales Area Managers** Laura Zuffova, Sabrina Ahmed, Bryan Anes, Simon Reddy
**Digital Sales Manager** Rola Touffaha
**Business Development Manager** Pouneh Hafizi

**Director of Retail** Ivan Rodrigues
**Retail Sales Coordinator** Michelle Mascarenhas
**Retail Sales Area Supervisors** Ahmed Mainodin, Firos Khan
**Retail Sales Merchandisers** Johny Mathew, Shan Kumar, Mehmood Ullah
**Retail Sales Drivers** Shabsir Madathil, Nimicias Arachchige
**Warehouse Assistants** Mohamed Haji, Jithinraj M

### Finance, HR & Administration
**Accountant** Cherry Enriquez
**Accounts Assistants** Sunil Suvarna, Jeanette Enecillo
**Administrative Assistant** Joy San Buenaventura
**Reception** Jayfee Manseguiao
**Public Relations Officer** Rafi Jamal
**Office Assistant** Shafeer Ahamed
**Office Manager – India** Jithesh Kalathingal

### IT & Digital Solutions
**Web Developers** Mirza Ali Nasrullah, Waqas Razzaq
**HTML/UI Developer** Naveed Ahmed
**IT Manager** R. Ajay
**Database Programmer** Pradeep T.P.

# Contact Us

### ▶ **Website**
Check out our new website for event listings, competitions and information on your city, and other cities in the Middle East.
Log onto ask**explorer**.com

### ▶ **Newsletter**
Register online to receive Explorer's newsletter and be first in line for our special offers and competitions.
Log onto ask**explorer**.com

### ▶ **General Enquiries**
We'd love to hear your thoughts and answer any questions you have about this book or any other Explorer product.
Contact us at info@ask**explorer**.com

### ▶ **Careers**
If you fancy yourself as an Explorer, send your CV (stating the position you're interested in) to jobs@ask**explorer**.com

### ▶ **Contract Publishing**
For enquiries about Explorer's Contract Publishing arm and design services, contact contracts@ask**explorer**.com

### ▶ **Maps**
For cartography enquiries, including orders and comments, contact maps@ask**explorer**.com

### ▶ **Advertising and Corporate Sales**
For bulk sales and customisation options, for this book or any Explorer product, contact sales@ask**explorer**.com

# Useful Numbers

## Emergency Services

| | |
|---|---|
| **Emergency Services** (Police, Fire, Ambulance) | 999 |
| **Electricity & Water Emergency** | 991 |
| **Vehicle Recovery** (Arabian Allied Association) | 4413 0970 |

## Airport Info

| | |
|---|---|
| **Hamad International Airport:** | |
| Lost & Found | 4010 5578 |
| Enquiries | 4010 6666 |
| **Airport Immigration/Passport Control** | 4462 1751 |

## Directory

| | |
|---|---|
| **Directory Assistance** | 180 |
| **Qatar International Dialling Code** | +974 |
| **Weather Information** | 4465 6590 |

## Taxi Operators

| | |
|---|---|
| **Karwa Taxis** | 4458 8888 |

## Limousine Operators

| | |
|---|---|
| **Doha Limousine** | 4483 9999 |
| **Elite Limousine** | 4442 6184 |
| **Fox Limousine** | 4462 2777 |
| **Qatar Limousine** | 4468 8688 |